Finding
Happiness

Finding Happiness

A Path to Self Acceptance

J. Patricia Gileno

Dedication

For my family. Gavin, my husband who supports me in everything I do, no matter how big or crazy my ideas are and giving me the courage to do something as crazy as sharing my life story! You never hold me back, instead you give me the kick I need to push myself to do more. You make me brave! To my son, who has the most genuine and kindest soul I have ever seen, known as the "walking heart." I learn so much from you every day! And to my daughter, whose independence, confidence, and creativity is an inspiration. I can't wait to see you kick ass in life.

To Jaime, my sounding board during this process and a fellow survivor!

To my publisher Sanjay, for taking a chance on me. And to my editor, Barbara, who I feel like we were meant to meet and work on this together.

Thank you all for supporting me through my roller coaster of emotions, ideas, and craziness! I hope I make you all proud!

To my readers; Thank you for picking up this book. Let's lift each other up as we are all survivors!

Disclaimer: This book is my interpretation of things that have happened in my life.

Contents

Part 3
What Is In Your Control?
Self Improvement

Introduction

If my own mom doesn't love me, then I must be unlovable and not worth love. This is a thought that I have struggled with for my whole life. My Mom never liked me and always thought of me as "bad." Every time something good would happen in my life, my Mom would be mad and remind me of how she felt about me which was never positive. My happiness caused her unhappiness and she would try to sabotage anything good that happened to me. Leading to the question of, why? I suspect my Mother has Narcissistic Personality Disorder, but I only came to this realization in my late thirties. And I lived my whole life thinking I was a terrible person because my Mom said so.

We are taught that a mom's love is unconditional. They are there to love you, guide you, be your cheering squad and safety net in life. So, what happens when this is not the case? What happens if your mom criticizes you all the time, puts you down and talks negatively about you to others? And your Dad and extended family do not step in to protect you? Well, I can tell you. You start believing it! That is what happened to me, as I felt like no matter what I did, it was never good enough. Regardless of any compliments I received from other people, I could not believe them because my Mother thought the opposite or would call them liars.

"Wow you seem so normal for what you've been through!" Is usually the reply I would get if I shared personal stories about my upbringing. I used to treat this as the highest compliment that I could receive as I worked hard to put on a happy face, be perfect and put on a good show regardless of how I was feeling inside. Now I realize, pretending to be "normal" is not healthy, not real and what is "normal" anyway? Are any of us truly "normal"? No, we are human. We are complex, imperfect and that makes us unique. In a world of social media showing us everyone's perfect lives, it makes it harder to be real. But embracing who you truly are (the good and the bad) is freeing and the best thing you can do for yourself.

As I child, I didn't realize how bad things were or how I was living wasn't normal or healthy. It's all I knew. Growing older I realized I experienced abuse and bullying from a narcissist. The more I read and researched, the more I realized that there are a lot of us victims out there and whatever we go through, we all have a choice. We do not have to live like a victim or use our experiences as a reason not to try to have a better life. There will be external factors that will affect us, but at the end of the day how we react is up to us and we can work to be in control of our own life!

I find a Mother-Daughter relationship to be very complicated. If you have a toxic person in your life, you're encouraged to remove them to protect your mental health and usually told supportive things like, "you're worth more." When it comes to being raised by a toxic Mom or family, you are persuaded to make it work. Why? Because she's your mom. No matter how bad things got with my Mom, I was pressured to find a way to make it work and it was my responsibility to fix our relationship (not hers). I finally said good-bye to my Mom six years ago. It was a decision most people didn't understand because (a) I always tried to act "normal" and happy, so people didn't realize how bad things were and (b) she's my Mom. Society doesn't equip kids with the tools needed or provide support to kids growing up in environments that are not healthy. Whatever our experiences, she's the Mom . . . therefore she is right.

I promise to be open and embarrassingly honest in sharing my stories and research to give advice on how to overcome challenging upbringings. I will cover a lot about Narcissistic Personality Disorders, but will also review bullying, abuse and how to cope.

This book is laid out in three phases to help you, the reader, find self-acceptance.

1. Recognizing when situations are not about you and not in your control. This is to clear space to focus on what you can control or do to improve in your life.
2. Identify what happened to you so you know where you need help.
3. Focusing on you, what is in your control and self-improvement.

I hope it will help you realize that whatever brought you here is for a reason and will help you start healing and finding your own happiness.

This book has been quite the journey! I started it thinking I knew everything about what I went through and I was so enthusiastic about writing it! Over the year it took to complete, I realized that we are never done learning and every day is a new lesson. There were times when writing it almost broke me. It really forced me to look at my life and acknowledge everything I've been through. The biggest lesson I've learned is that the more self-aware you are, the stronger you will become. I hope this book does the same for you and makes you a stronger person and think the craziest thought ever . . . that you are worth being happy!

Before we dig in, I want you to write on a piece of paper what made you pick up this book. Save it and revisit at the end. You may think you picked this book up for one reason, but as we're constantly learning about ourselves and evolving, I bet by the end of the book your reason will be more complex but will be filled with hope and direction.

Good luck to you and your journey! I hope this book will be the first step in changing your life for the better and that it can help you forgive the people that hurt you and be more open to an amazing life! I hope this helps you take control of your life, kick ass, find happiness and your path to self-acceptance! LET'S DO THIS!!!!

Part One

Sometimes It's Just Not About You!

Chapter 1

Recognize When Situations are Not About You or In Your Control

Childhood is a monumental time in life as it begins to shape who you are and can have a big effect on whom you become. During this time, you learn many life skills such as how to love, share, and trust. As a child, you don't decide what to eat, where you are going or even what school you attend. So, if we weren't in control of anything in our childhood, why do we blame ourselves for things that happened?

In order to take charge of your life, the first step is to be aware of what you can't control in your past, present and future. Think of it as removing the noise on your healing journey. Your childhood is a prime example of when you didn't have control as you depended on your parents to care for you. While the majority of this book will discuss how you can control your life, the first step is acknowledging and being able to identify instances in your life that have nothing to do with you. Isolate incidents where you couldn't have changed your experience no matter how you reacted. As an adult there will also be cir-cumstances that are not in your control, however the difference is you can control how you react and how they impact you. This chapter is going to focus on things not in your control so you can start healing and focusing on things that are. Childhood is a big part of this.

Identifying what is not in your control will make room for you to focus what you can control and help you to move on. Realizing that parts of my childhood were not because of me, was free-ing and helped me move forward and be more aware of how I react to situations. As an example, because my Mom had me convinced that nobody liked me, I had this perception that nobody really did. Realizing that a normal loving, mom would never say anything like that to her child, and realizing that these thoughts were in my head because of my childhood, I was able to look at my future interactions differently and open my mind and heart to new relationships.

Maybe there are elements in your life where you were a victim but not because of anything you did. We are going to start building the foundation to get you to the next steps to those things that you can control in your life. Let's start reducing the noise!

Remember when you were a child and you believed everything had to do with you, and your ultimate goal was to make your parents, teachers or person of authority, happy. You do all you can to please them and if they are happy, then you are happy and feel fulfilled. As a parent it doesn't matter what sort of day you had, or that something serious happened. If you're not showing your child a happy face, they think, "what did I do to upset Mom." As a child you trust your family and parents, as it's all you know. They are the first people you meet, and love and they are there to raise and guide you through life. Being a part of a family and respecting your family is what you have been taught and is how society views family units. At school you are taught about families, to celebrate occasions like Mother's Day. Your mom specifically is your first love. She is the first person you meet and is your lifeline. Her happiness is her child's world! Her empathy and reaction to our feelings, needs, and wants, help shape us into who we are.

People generally don't discuss when things are wrong at home or educate kids in ways to cope. At least in my life there wasn't. Growing up we were taught that parents are always right. What happens if you were brought into this world under difficult circumstances? If you weren't wanted or if you were a product of a broken relationship? If your Mom is mad at you or if family members walk away, you immediately think, "what did I do wrong." Being a child is such a fragile time of your life as you are 100% reliant on your family to guide you, coach you, love you. When your family is not supportive or nurturing, what happens? When your family does not show love, how do you cope and thrive?

My entire childhood was a constant thought of "what did I do wrong?" and being envious of kids at school where I would see parents volunteering and outwardly showing love for their children. I always felt out of place, not like I was loved or wanted. I felt like I was a nuisance, consumed with the thought, am I a bad person? I believed I must've been, because my Mom made me feel that way.

My Mom was seldom happy. She was a small woman in height and weight, average looking with brown hair and eyes, and had a constant "hard" look, rarely smiling. She usually looked unapproachable, but the odd times she did smile, I thought she looked beautiful. Her smile, to me, showed that I did something right. I cherished these small wins. She had a hard childhood and would reference this all the time as a way to excuse her behavior and to also make me feel silly whenever I was upset, for she always had had it worse than me. Her hard childhood was a tool used for sympathy and the reason for her bad behaviors. It was also used to belittle how I was feeling, to dismiss it, making me feel stupid. While she acknowledged she had a tough childhood, she was never wrong and never admitted she needed professional help.

She viewed herself as different and better than everyone, and was very opinionated, always having reasons for not liking somebody. There were many times when she wouldn't like someone and felt they were judging her or giving her a bad feeling. On top of all of this, according to her, she had a psychic ability, so when I would question these "feelings" she would say that it's her "gift." This "gift" would limit her interactions with people and alienate our family from others as there was always a negative feeling. This included extended family and was part of the reason we moved around a lot. My Mom didn't get along with many people, so I didn't have a strong support system with my immediate family or extended family as they weren't around much.

My Mom made me feel like I wasn't enough, hardly ever showed affection and constantly put me down. Growing up I would think, why is my Mom not happy with me and why do I keep losing people from my life? I felt misplaced and like I was an uninvited guest in my own home. It affected my whole life and made me feel like I wasn't good enough and that I needed to make myself small and be invisible. I felt the need to please people and put on the happy act, while staying out of the way and fading into the background. The older I grew, the smaller I felt. Typically, moms show love, empathy, and want the best for their kids. When they don't, is there more going on? It is human nature to think situations are about you, but the freedom in realizing that sometimes it isn't, can be life changing and the beginning of the healing process to controlling your life.

I met my real Dad when I was five years old, however, I didn't even know he was my Dad until years later. The only thing that I knew about this man was that he was a quiet, awkward man who would take me to McDonalds on Sundays. He was tall, had big blue eyes, brown hair, and a thick bushy mustache. He was very quiet and would make awkward small talk with me. And a lot of the time he would just stare with those big blue eyes making me uncomfortable (ironically, I have his eyes. Something my Mom hated and would consistently tell me). We didn't seem to have much in common and wouldn't have a lot to talk about so I would focus on my Happy Meal and my love for cheeseburgers.

My Mom absolutely hated this man and introduced him to me as a "distant loser uncle." I hated these Sundays. Not because of anything my Dad/distant loser uncle did. It was how my Mom treated me leading up to them. She would get angry every weekend knowing this McDonalds visit was coming. She would stomp around the house, get mad at the littlest things and would criticize me for not getting angry along with her, all the while going on a rant about how terrible a man he was. As a five-year-old, it was incredibly confusing. All I wanted was to make her happy which I tried to do twice as much on these Sundays. I didn't understand if she hated this "terrible man" so much why was I forced to see him weekly? Why was she mad at me on these Sundays, when she was the one forcing me to go? Way too complicated for a young child and I did the only thing I thought was right. I hated him too, to please my Mom and acted like I didn't even like McDonalds Happy Meals anyways.

It was a couple of years later, when I learned the truth of who this man was, my actual Dad, which only further confused me. I still didn't understand what was going on? Any time I asked my Mom, she would get angry, so I stopped asking.

You see, while eventually she did tell me the truth about the "distant loser uncle's" identity, it was followed by years of many harsh and disturbing stories. She would tell me stories of him beating her, almost forcing her to have an abortion while pregnant with me (which then led to her having to explain what abortion meant as I was too young to understand), and trying to kidnap me, etc. Disclaimer: I will say this is all alleged and my Mom tends to exaggerate for attention to ensure people take her side. All stories told would make her the hero. I still don't know the truth to this day. Yet for some reason I had to see him every Sunday and every Sunday I would take the heat from her tempers for the occasion, and every Sunday I tiptoed around her. If I even smiled by accident it would turn into a war with accusations of me taking his side. Turns out these Sunday visits were due to the custody agreement. I'm not sure why they started when I was five. Maybe he wasn't interested in getting to know me until later, questioning if I was his child or maybe dealing with my Mom was too much. Like I said, too complicated for a child, however I felt it the worst and really it had nothing to do with me. I couldn't help being born! But I felt like this was 100% my fault and constantly felt guilty because of it.

At school when we would make crafts to bring home to our mom and dads, I would never say anything. I would dread the days when I needed to bring the "dad" crafts home because I never knew what to do with them. On good days I would have the opportunity to throw them in the garbage. I would hate, hate, hate Father's Day. I would create the craft with a pit in my stomach and just pray that I could find a garbage bin to discard it, without being caught. There was one time when I couldn't get rid of it, and it was one of my worst days. I was berated for doing a good job on my Father's Day gift and questioned why I didn't put as much thought or care into her Mother's Day gift a month earlier. I hated all parental occasions. They were always filled with drama and rage!

Badmouthing and these forced visits went on for years, further confusing me about relationships and parents. I tried to be polite, make everyone happy and even tried to get them to like each other but the hatred never dulled from my Mom. My Dad never said anything negative about her to me, and I didn't ask any questions until much later as I still felt guilt for having to have these Sundays with him, so I stayed as quiet as possible. These Sundays continued and we would sit in McDonalds in awkward silence. I could never shake how I made Mom so mad when I went to my Dads, and I felt so guilty.

There was an occasional visit to his house, and although we saw each other weekly, we didn't truly develop a relationship. I was guarded and felt that if I did open up, it would betray my Mom. We never had an honest conversation and never really got to know each other, our relationship was on the surface and forced.

Things came to an explosive peak with my Dad and I, when my Mom threw me out of the house at the age of fifteen. I was forced to live with my Dad which was incredibly confusing as according to her he was enemy number 1. He had his own family; two kids with a wife who was not happy about me or this arrangement of me living with her family. My Dad traveled a lot for work, so it was usually just the kids and her with me, an additional child to look after. When my Dad wasn't around,

I was greeted with a ten-page list of rules written by his wife that needed to be followed at all times. These rules ranged from things like; don't eat food without asking and don't touch anything that isn't mine (which was basically everything). The last rule was the worst and one that I will never forget. It read something along the lines of, "Never think that this is your house. This is not your house or your family, you are a guest. A guest that was not invited." She treated me terribly when my Dad wasn't around, which was often. When he was present, she treated me like one of her own and everything was perfect with her playing the perfect Step-Mom.

My sixteenth birthday is when everything exploded and became the beginning of the end. She planned a birthday party for me filled with decorations, birthday cake . . . it was so beautiful and to an outsider looking in, so thoughtful. However this party was completely and disgustingly fake. It was all a show for my Dad. It was so obviously a show that my half-brother who was around nine at the time even said something like—Mom did you make a mistake? It's Jennie's birthday. I went through the motions of smiling for the camera and saying thank you for the presents and gave the family hugs. But really, I knew that this was an

act and I was so over it. I needed love and acceptance, not presents. Picture getting a Nintendo
game for your birthday. From afar it looks like a
great and cool gift, but in reality, you don't own a
console or have a home and only own the clothes
you brought in an old used grocery bag.

As soon as it was over, I asked my Dad to talk
privately. It was like something clicked in me and
I couldn't take it anymore. I couldn't believe how
clueless he was, and I finally got the courage to
confront him on everything. I laid it all out there,
everything that I had ever been told and asked him
for the truth. The stories, my Mom's accusations,
the treatment of his wife, all of it that I had been
storing up for sixteen years of my life, finally spoken. This was his opportunity to tell me something,
anything, show some sort of emotion towards
me! Did he ever really want me? I so desperately
needed somebody to want to me and care about
me. Did he try to force my Mom to get an abortion?
Did he try to "beat me out of her?" Does he realize that I need to follow ten pages of rules to live
with him? I was so desperate to hear even a tiny,
subtle hint that he fought for me and lost . . . something! I was a starving child, looking for a crumb
of reassurance. Anything to make me feel wanted
by somebody, and you know what I got . . . nothing!

Now at sixteen, I was pretty mature for my age after all that I had been through, so it's not like I was hoping that it would be like they show in the movies, when the kid finds their long last Dad and there's a secret drawer of letters or birthday cards showing that he really cared about me all these years. But I really, desperately wanted something! At this point in my life, I had no family. Him and his family were it. What was his response? Nothing! There wasn't a reaction, more of a speechless approach. He didn't really say anything just awkwardly stuttered as he drank his beer. At the lowest, low of my life I was expecting something, desperate for any sort of reaction. Anger at the lies, confirmation that they were indeed lies, fight to make me believe he did love me . . . something! Instead? Nothing . . . I ran away that night with nowhere to go and no plan! All I knew is that I didn't want to live in yet another house where I wasn't wanted and was tired of the constant feeling of guilt and feeling like nobody loved me or wanted me in their life. Nobody chased after me.

I look back on this time in my life and think to myself, what really happened or was this truly it and that he didn't care? Did I simply catch my Dad off guard, did he realize all of the horrifying stories I've been told by my Mom over the years? Did he realize that I was only a "guest" in his house following ten pages of rules? Did he even want me to stay at his house or even want me in his life? Truth is, I don't know. Nor will I ever know. I found out years later that he's possibly an alcoholic. Maybe he was too drunk to understand everything that I was going through? Or was it simply that the relationship was doomed from the beginning, tainted by my Mom and he thought that I hated him? I was trained to hate this man and if I ever had fun or did like him, I felt like I was betraying my Mom and had to hide my joy. Her making me live with him was so confusing. I still had that sense of loyalty that I can't like him, or she'll be mad at me even though she forced me to stay with him. When he didn't fight for me, it made me believe that maybe my Mom was right. Maybe he was the loser she described him to be and maybe I truly was unlovable. How could I think anything else? One parent kicked me out. The other showed no emotion whatsoever!

His lack of reaction caused me to run away from his house and become homeless for the first time. This wouldn't be the last time I would be a homeless teenager however, it was the scariest time as I had no idea what I was doing or how I was going to go on. It was also the first time I contemplated if life was worth living as I truly felt alone and unwanted. Even worse, I felt like nobody would care if I died and if I did die, then at least I was out of everyone's way and it would make everyone's life easier. I ended up staying at a few friends' houses for a few weeks and eventually moved back home to my Mom's, until the next time I was kicked out and homeless again.

Another layer in my complicated family dynamic is that I also have a step-dad who came into my life about a year before my real Dad entered. My Step-Dad was very tall, kind with friendly blue eyes and light brown wavy hair. The best way to describe him was simple. He was pretty easy-going at the beginning and the teller of typical dad jokes. He was a caretaker for the school board, had hobbies of wood working and very rarely formed his own opinions. He just went with the flow. He was like a piece of clay. My Mom could mold him into what she wanted, and he echoed her opinions. Perfect! She wore the pants in their relationship and as the years went on his small voice kept getting smaller. Over the years he too turned hard and into a meaner version of himself with the biggest goal of "not getting involved" in anything to do with me and would turn a blind eye to the treatment I would receive from my Mom. When he entered our lives, there were no real introductions. One day he showed up at our apartment and never left. The day he moved in I was so scared I almost called 911 as I thought he was breaking in because I had never met him before. This tall man just entered our apartment and started hugging my Mom, which I perceived as attacking her. Turns out he was coming to live with us permanently, without warning or introductions.

Being a parent now, I would think that the proper thing is to sit their child down and explain the situation, have them meet prior to living together but that didn't happen for me. Within a year I had met a "distant loser Uncle/Dad" and my Mom's boyfriend who was moving in and who I thought was robbing our apartment on our first encounter. When he moved in, our family dynamic shifted again, and my new role was being used as a tool for my mom to get sympathy from my Step-Dad. She would exaggerate things I did or get mad at me for the silliest things, then retreat to my Step-Dad for sympathy and support. An example was my first day of kinder-school. I screamed and cried at drop-off and I tore the teacher's stockings in the middle of my temper tantrum. This story was told a lot, as I embarrassed her terribly and it was a great story to get sympathy from my Step-Dad. Behind the scenes was the first car ride to the daycare where I was lectured and yelled at for always embarrassing her and she wanted to make sure that I wouldn't do that again (turns out I did . . . by acting like a kid). My Mom enjoyed the hero role for raising me, needing sympathy while I was the bad kid who was a burden.

When he moved in, I remember I would hate to wake up in the morning and would spend most days in my room to avoid them. She would criticize every little thing and complain to him to the point where I hated doing anything and wished so hard to be invisible. I was great for their relationship because she got so much attention from him for raising such a terrible child.

I was not allowed a real relationship with my Step-Dad. Anytime it would look like we were getting along she would pull me aside and remind me that he isn't my real Dad. She would tell me things like, it wasn't appropriate for him to play with me or tickle me or that he's only playing with me to make my Mom happy, he's just being polite and doesn't really like me. When he would get mad at me, she would whisper to me out of his earshot, "I told you he doesn't like you!" She would convince me that she was trying to get him to like me, but

I kept being bad so it was impossible for anyone, other than her, to like me. I could not understand how I was being bad though, because all I would try to do is hide, even missing meals so I didn't have to interact with them.

With inheriting a Step-Dad, I got to be a part of his side of the family and they were great. I had a lot of new cousins that were around the same age, so whenever family get togethers would happen we would all play together and have a blast. It was tough to hide how much I liked them as we all got along so well and always had so much fun together and my Mom didn't like my getting along with his family. She would remind me in private that they were his family and not mine, saying, "They don't really like you" and "You're making a fool out of yourself by playing with them, because they make fun of you when you leave." It really hurt every time she told me that they were just pretending to like me because they were being polite. She would tell me things like this a lot, making me hesitant to form relationships with this family.

It was the same when I was making a new friend or building a relationship, she would add "But you know I am only one that will tell you the truth as I am your Mom. They're just pretending to like you to be polite," and lastly, "I'm the only one who likes you because I have to, since I'm your Mom." It made me second guess friendships and feel foolish when I would be happy playing with people and having fun. It was a heavy weight of fear, thinking nobody liked me and an even heavier weight thinking everyone makes fun of me when I'm not around. I thought I must be a terrible person that doesn't deserve love. As nobody likes me, my Mom also doesn't like me, however, she's the only one there for me despite of how bad I am. Picture a child trying to digest all of this at the age of five.

She would criticize my Step-Dad's family heavily. Calling them everything from losers to pathetic. As they grew older they were bums, fatties and losers that would never amount to anything (the word loser was frequently used, it was her favorite word to describe people. She loved that word!). It was constant name calling from her, she really hated them and as I'm her daughter (only hers), I was supposed to be on her side in these judgments. There were times, when she treated these rants as confiding in me, which made me feel special like maybe she does love me. I was so hungry for love I would take anything. Plus, there was this deep down feeling of, well if they hate me and make fun of me, then her calling them names made me feel a little better. Do you remember being a kid and having so much fun, you would lose track of time and forget the world? That's the level of fun I would have with these cousins but when the playing was over, the over-whelming guilt would set in. Feelings of betrayal, shame and thinking they were only pretending to have fun playing with me. This started around the age of five and continued way into my thirties. As I got older and started to know better, I would try to defend them, which was the hardest thing to do because it usually meant getting berated with insults for months to years for being stupid and not seeing through those losers and for defending people who weren't my real family.

When it came to family, I felt like I had no one, and I don't belong anywhere. And if I needed help, it was horrible, and met with negative comments such as, "The world does not revolve around you," or "How you can be so selfish," and the most com-mon, "No wonder people don't like you." This envi-ronment was so toxic.

Relationships and friendships were hard for me. It was a tug of war of emotions. Do they really like me or are they pretending to because I'm bad? Does my Mom like them (Ha! Never!)?

Will my Mom get mad? I would desperately want the relationships, but I would be too scared to fully commit to them. One time in Grade 5 I let my guard down. I made a best friend, Kristi, and we were inseparable. We wanted to be together 24/7. This would be my first best friend. We had so many similar interests, would always want to play together and when apart, would beg our parents to let us go to each other's house. My mom, seeing this friendship getting so strong, interfered and told me that Kristi was only pretending to like me and was laughing about me behind my back with the other girls in our class. (Apparently my Mom somehow saw it). To please my Mom, I ended the friendship right there, with no explanation, and feeling like such a fool. I'll never forget the day I ran into Kristi's Mom at the school and got the dirtiest look. I couldn't understand why. Now looking back, I'm assuming I hurt my friend and that she was not doing all the things my Mom said she was. This is one story of many relationships my Mom would sabotage. My Mom never liked me having anyone in my life.

Another relationship that was complicated was my relationship with food. My parents were very odd when it came to food. My brother was born shortly after my Mom and Step-Dad got together and growing up, I pretty much raised him as I was seven years older. To me, he was my baby. My brother's goal was to just to fit in, but he always had trouble. He was blonde with brown eyes, very cute, a little on the heavier side and full of opinions that he learned from my Mom. He was a little person with adult opinions and as such was bullied. He had an easier home life than I did, but still tough for an average child. Food was something that we both struggled with as my parents would comment on how much we were eating, and lock up most of the food from us. Starting in Grade 5, I would watch my brother often. I would walk him to and from school when he was in kindergarten, and I would have to watch him home alone until my parents got back from work. We would come home from school starving and as food was locked up, I had to get creative in how I could feed my brother. They would sometimes not lock up cereal or bread so we would carefully snack on these. We were careful because there were times when my parents would mark where the cereal was filled in a box, and notice if we touched any dishes. It got so bad, that my parents ended up dedicating a room in the basement where food would be kept under lock and key.

When I got my first job, all I did was eat! I would buy food with my paychecks and hoard it in my room. Food would be junk food, fruit, SpaghettiOs (long expiration dates) and I would sneak it to my brother. Now just to be clear, my parents would feed us but the bare minimum of three meals a day and no snacks. She would be very observant of my weight and comment if she felt I ate too much and if she felt I had gained too much weight. I remember around the age of ten, my Step-Dad would have a bag of change for poker that he kept on his dresser. I would steal change to buy food for my brother and I. I got caught stealing and when I tried to explain I was buying food, it only made things worse. I was grounded to my room for a week (only allowed to leave to use the washroom at certain times). How this impacted me as an adult was, it made me sensitive to the food available and caused the occasional overindulgence. I would dream of one day having my own apartment . . . and a whole box of Viva Puffs (which I did buy when I moved out). I would dream about food constantly. I had a fear of being hungry and not having my next meal.

The common theme of these stories is I couldn't understand what was happening and all I wanted was for my Mom to be happy and to like me. I just desperately longed to feel wanted and assured I wasn't a bad person. I was constantly blaming myself for things that weren't in my control and trying to be the person my Mom wanted without ever really knowing or accomplishing that goal. Often throughout childhood I questioned why people kept leaving me and why do things always happen to me? A lot of the losses I outlined, weren't about me. I was a child looking up and trusting my Mom because she was my Mom! We are taught that family is supposed to protect, love and want their children. In my case, my Mom was not doing things in my best interest and was making me not trust the world. She was training me to only trust her, and as she didn't really think I was a good person, I believed it. Growing up this way was a form of abuse and as I got older, I learned, it was not about me. None of this could have been about me, I was only a child!

It took years to learn this and years to forgive myself for being that terrible person she thought I was. More importantly, I finally realized that I actually was not that terrible person she made me feel I was. I was a child. A child that loved her Mom and all she wanted was the love and acceptance returned. That realization made me feel lighter looking back on my childhood. And gave me some freedom from my past. While your childhood shapes the foundation of who you become, it does not have to define you permanently. Taking a look at your childhood objectively, can give you a different perspective and can help determine what was not in your control. I could not control that I was born into a world where my parents hated each other, and I was never really wanted. I suffered because of a life that they created and in reality, none of these instances had anything to do with me. I could not control my Mother's hatred.

Removing this noise can make room for the things that you can control and change in your life. In your path of self-improvement, it's important to acknowledge all you have been through, but realize the things that were not in your control. Try to minimize the time spent on blaming yourself for things that you couldn't control in order to make room to focus on things you can. For example, how you react to things because of how you were raised. While your childhood can scar, chances are there isn't much you could have done to change things so it's best to look at childhood as how it shaped you and if there are scars, how can we fix now? We'll visit this in later chapters.

Chapter 2

Bullying, Finding the Strength

I went to a total of seven schools by Grade 9 . . . yes, you read that right! We know that building a foundation or creating a village for a child is so important, but my Mom for some reason always wanted to move "for a change of scenery." Looking back, I think she might have been moving to get away from people that she got into a fight with as she caused conflict wherever she went. I was simply along for the ride. We moved around so much, that there were schools where I stopped trying to make friends entirely. I figured that making friends would mean (a) they would laugh about me behind my back or (b) since we would move anyway it was not worth it, as I didn't want to miss them. One year, I tried to pretend that I was someone better than the real me. Rich, stylish and I had many toys. It's pretty funny as we lived in a dingy apartment building, but I was so used to moving around and losing people in my life that I started to play with different personas. I was never mean to anyone, but I did have a strong personality when I wanted. While I stopped trying to make friends and did my own thing, my brother tried so desperately to make friends. He would vocalize "his" (My Mom's) opinions on people, but would get nervous of people's reactions as he was so desperate to fit in. This nervous personality caused a tick. When he would get nervous, he would make a funny duck sound while sticking out his jaw, so it was very prevalent. When I heard of him being bullied, I would go to defend him. This would mean sneaking on to the school yard where the younger kids were and confronting the mean kids. I'm not sure if this made things better or worse for my brother, but I didn't hear of too many instances afterwards.

While my brother was bullied a lot over the years, I did not experience bullying until Grade 9. I did such a great job of being invisible but the day my appearance changed, I became center of attention, in the worst way. I was bullied severely and skipped school often with almost ninety absences that single year. I had an extreme case of an overactive thyroid and it affected my appearance. An overactive thyroid is when your body works overtime because it is producing too much of the thyroid hormone, and everything in your body is functioning at a high speed. My heart raced, I had heart palpitations, I was always tired with brain fog, and felt exhausted 24/7. I was about 80 lbs (at the age of 14, the average weight is approximately 100–120 lbs), had lost a lot of my hair creating bald spots in patches and had really large eyes that looked like they were bulging out of my eye sockets.

As if life wasn't hard enough, I had this boy who was a year older than me who would never stop picking on me. You might be picturing a large, tall overbearing presence of a boy since he was a bully, however he couldn't be more different. He was shorter than my 5'1" height, skinny but so loud and obnoxious. He would line up the halls with people near my locker and get everyone to call me "bug eyes" at every opportunity possible. I would dread walking down any hallway as I never knew when I would need to walk through this extremely embarrassing case of bullying. When there weren't lines of people shouting "bug eyes," people would randomly shout it as I would walk by or shout it into my classroom for all to hear.

Sometimes they would throw garbage at me, try to trip me or "accidentally" run into me so I would drop my books.

I was too weak to defend myself, which made me an even bigger target. I tried to figure out ways to avoid the "hot spots" where I knew these bullies would be, but they always found me. I found out later that they learned my schedule and would plan their day accordingly. It was so humiliating and mortifying, that I would wish to move again, but high school was when I stayed in one place for the longest duration (ironic, right?). I lost so many friends, people didn't want to be associated with me, my boyfriend broke up with me and to make matters worse, my Mom thought I was making stories up for attention and didn't want to hear anything about the torture I was experiencing. To her, I was an attention seeker and exaggerated stories "because the world always needed to revolve around Jennie," and that I needed to "learn the lesson that the world doesn't revolve around me." Grade 9 was my hardest time at school.

In late Grade 10 and early Grade 11, I started to overcome my illness and began to be able to function. My hair started growing back and my eyes returning to normal, I started thinking more clearly and had more energy. But the damage had been done and I had trouble trusting the kids that tried to re-enter my life. Even that boyfriend who broke up with me tried to get back together (seriously?).

To say I hated life, was an understatement. I hated everything about my life, but because I had the constant brain fog, I don't think I was even processing everything properly. I remember going to bed each night and wishing I wouldn't wake up in the morning. I would love to tell you where I found the strength during this phase and tell you how I coped, but the reality is that I was too sick to fully process until my health turned around. The only thing I did do, was take each day on like a new one. Might sound funny, but in my mind looking at a full week of school was too overwhelming. I would only think day by day.

When my health started getting better, I would look back on this time and reflect. It taught me a lot about bullying, about teenagers, about caregivers and most of all, about myself. Teenagers just want to conform to the norm and will shy away from someone who is bullied or centered out. It's that fear of catching whatever is wrong with the victim or the fear of them being bullied themselves, i.e., if I become her friend, they will bully me too. It made me grow up even faster and made me aware of people who weren't genuine. My home life already made forming relationships difficult but bullying and being isolated also made me more wary of new people and their true intentions. High school is tough for anyone who is a little bit different, but with the proper support at home, it can be easier. Always support your kids, friends' kids, any kids for that matter. No problem is too small to deserve your attention and your guidance. As for caregivers, yes you should be able to depend on teachers, counselors etc., however, there are some crappy ones out there so don't let them stall your progress or healing. Ultimately, you are in control of your own life, so if something doesn't feel right, it probably isn't. Try not to let it slow you down.

Researching for this chapter, I had no idea how big of a problem bullying is, and how secretive kids can be about it. It can be heartbreaking. Not only are children getting hurt by bullying, but also from the shame they feel from being the target. What stood out the most to me was the disconnect between students and their teachers.

Here are some stats—According to the Canadian Red Cross, 71% of teachers say that they usually intervene with bullying, yet students say only 25% of teachers intervene. Teachers only see 4%

of the bullying that occurs, and students report bullying only 30% of the time. Depending on who answered these questions, the student or the teacher, these are big variances.

The reason for the discrepancy is simple. Children who are bullied feel ashamed and try to hide it, or they feel if they tell someone it will only get worse and the bullying will increase. So how do you identify if someone is being bullied and just how big is this problem? According to the Canadian Red Cross, a study showed in thirty-three Toronto junior high schools, 49.5% of their school population had been bullied. Basically, half of the student population had been bullied at some point of their school life. You would hope that in an age where we have information at our fingertips and an increased awareness to bullying, children would experience it less and adults would be more aware. The unfortunate reality is that kids today are experiencing bullying online for all to see, further amplifying this torture.

The study also states that 70% of students are reported to have been bullied online and 44% of students have admitted to being bullies. These stats are astounding. The challenge for a parent as to stay as connected to your child, as children are ashamed and they keep it a secret. I share these stats to show that if you have been bullied, you are not alone. There are way too many of us! Sometimes, there is comfort in knowing there are other survivors out there.

Victims of bullying show signs ranging from a loss of interest in school activities, lower grades, and skipping school. Victims also demonstrate feelings of isolation, loneliness and depression. If a child is being bullied, they may not be social but withdrawn.

What do you picture when you hear the word bully? Do you picture a larger child yelling at a smaller child, stealing their money, making fun of their appearance? It gets a little more complicated than that, especially now with social media. According to Google, the definition of bullying is a physical or verbal aggression that is repeated with the intent on being mean and instilling power over another. Usually something causes these bullies to act out, for example, their homelife may be challenged, or they have unresolved feelings of neglect etc. This could explain the reason bullies need to feel powerful and pick on someone who is less strong or is different. What is the easiest way to hide your insecurity? Find someone who looks like they are weaker than you and deflect the attention to the weaker person.

Bystanders also have a key role in bullying. Bystanders of bullies observe but do not step in to help the victim. Those who are too afraid to defend the victim for fear of being attacked themselves. Being witnesses to the bullying, they too keep quiet on the events taken place. Even though they are bystanders and technically not doing anything wrong, they could also be held accountable. I think of my Step-Dad who saw everything happen, but never stepped in and did anything. If he was only a bystander, does that make him innocent?

Sadly, almost half of us have experienced some form of bullying. You often hear advice such as "just ignore it" or "they're just jealous." This advice is counterproductive and can suppress the issue and encourage people to suffer in silence. I looked up advice for teens being bullied and it ranges from; ignore the bully, don't bully back, to stand up for yourself and tell an adult. A middle school or high school child's mentality is to conform and fit in, so their first instinct is to ignore and hope that it goes away. The best way to help children is to be supportive and be aware of any changes to behavior or reactions to school. Always ask, how was their day? Ask specific questions and try to be dialed into their life at school. Know who their friends are, how they feel about school.

For younger children, ask who made them laugh today, or who made them feel mad. If they have a stable support system at home, it will encourage them to talk about the events at school and can help you know when you need to step in. It will give them strength and a feeling of control to help them feel brave to take on the day.

Children who were bullied grow into adults and might experience a form of PTSD, have anxiety, feel paranoia, lack self-esteem and have difficulty trusting in people and forming relationships. In the later years of school, I got a part-time job which taught me so much and got me out of my high school and home bubbles. My part time job was at a fast food restaurant which employed mostly high school students and for the first time I learned what it felt like to have confidence, independence and I really started to learn social skills. For the first time I developed true friendships.

If you are in school and finding it tough, here are a few things to remember;

1. Only 15% of your life is in school. High school is only 5% (based on the average life expectancy of 79) While high school may seem like an eternity, try to remember only 5% or 4 years of your life will be spent there.

2. School is a small bubble in your life. Find other bubbles, whether it's a sport, part-time job or some sort of extra-curricular activity. The more bubbles you have, the less significant any one will be and the more well-rounded you will become. We may not always fit in, but the more bubbles we have, chances are, we will find where we belong.
3. If someone bullies you, it is not about you. Kind people do not bully.
4. Please, please, please confide in someone if you are being bullied. There is no need to suffer in silence and you are not alone. Like I said earlier almost 50% of people have been bullied. There are more like you out there.
5. Don't let anyone minimize your feelings. If someone is making you feel bad consistently, it is a form of bullying.

And lastly,

6. Find your passion in life and learn to love what makes you different. This is the hardest one by far and something I'm still trying to master to this day! You may never fully get there but, working towards a goal is something worth celebrating. Example, at my high school everyone made fun of the artists and called them "geeks." I hope all

those artists are still creating and are proud of their "differences."

There is no exact science as to how to persevere, but I hope these six points will help you feel better in your journey. The only thing that really kept me going was the thought, "I'll show them!" I wanted to prove to everyone that I wasn't the "bug eye freak" that people made me out to be and that drive got me to where I am today.

Bullying falls under this section as it's not about you. Kind, stable people do not want to inflict harm onto others and usually there is something more going on with the bully in question that has absolutely nothing to do with you. It's not up to you to diagnose what's wrong with the bully or why they act like this, however, it is up to you to realize that if you are bullied, it's not about you!

Part Two

What Happened to You? Identify So You Know Where You Need Help!

Chapter 3

What is NPD?

When I met my husband, life really moved forward at warp speed. We met, bought a house, and had a baby, all within the first year of knowing each other. It felt as though someone from above was saying, "Wow, finally they got their shit together and have met. Let's do this!" We were getting organized in our living arrangements, preparing for our little miracle to be born and I was sick 95% of the time from pregnancy symptoms. Saying things were hectic would be an understatement. This was the time when we needed support more than ever. So, this would be a perfect time for family to support us and help, right? WRONG! My Mom's erratic behavior went into hyper-drive, starting with my baby shower.

I did not want a baby shower. I worked for a toy company, so I received a lot of stuff from work, plus I was not feeling well, did not like all the fuss or attention, and lastly, a lot of my close friends are guys. I have never been a fan of baby showers. While I would attend those of my friends, I always knew I didn't want one. All I wanted was a small BBQ to celebrate. I was really looking forward to this idea as I hadn't seen a lot of my friends in months from being off sick. Everyone was ok with this idea, and some were relieved it was just a casual get together, except my Mom.

You would have thought that I told my Mom that I was going to set fire to her house, based on her reaction. Everything was a battle and a fight. I had to stop answering my phone. She was calling me so much about this baby shower that I would be in tears at work almost every morning. When I stopped answering my phone at work, she would have me paged saying that it was an emergency. I would get pulled out of meetings to talk to my Mom about having a baby shower and well, argue about everything! First, she wanted the baby shower at her house. But Gavin's family would not be invited, neither were my friends. Her reasoning? She didn't need a reason, it's her house! Then she wanted it at a hall but couldn't afford to contribute to the cost. And the list went on and on and on. She wasn't happy with the guest list as there were people on it that she didn't like (particularly my Step-Dad's family, especially his sister). She didn't think it was socially acceptable to have guys attend (I mean, what would people think?). Then she wasn't going because I didn't care about my baby's grandmother. To re-iterate, this was all during the time when I was nauseous day and night, working full-time, getting ready to move into a new house and preparing to have a baby.

My Mom never helped with any of it and anytime I asked for help, she was busy, or the response was, "I could help but if I don't help, it will make you a stronger person." The only thing she cared about was this baby shower that I didn't even want. It became all about her and gave me so much stress. To make her happy, I rented a party room close to her house so that it wasn't too far for her to drive to, did not invite guys, and asked my friends to help with the games. My Mom did not help because she was still upset at how I treated her. At the last minute she declined the invitation and said that she wasn't going because of my behavior. This was after I changed everything to give her the baby shower she wanted. After many phone calls consoling her and making her feel welcome, I convinced her to go by using one of my "go-tos." "Mom, how will I explain your absence?" i.e., "What will people think?" I continued planning what she wanted with no help from her what-so-ever. I had to pick her up, escort her and ensure that she wasn't sitting beside someone she didn't know or didn't like (specifically my Step-Dads family, I say this again because she was still very upset they were invited and used them as one of her excuses not to attend). She didn't bring a gift as she was going to buy us a crib instead but then decided we made too much money, so we didn't need her help. To be clear, we were ok that we didn't receive a gift, but I still think it's funny that she offered to buy us one of the more expensive things and then took it away as punishment for making too much money, in her opinion. (In reality we were broke from just buying the house and having maternity leave approaching).

This was typical. People are usually surprised when I tell stories like this, but for me this was everyday life and an embarrassing thing to try to explain to my significant other and his family. At the baby shower, she sulked and pouted when she didn't get any attention, criticized the entire thing and didn't lift a finger. Some people picked up on her behavior and would check-in on me. I just wanted the entire thing done with. I was so appreciative of everything that everyone had done, but I wasn't feeling well and just couldn't handle being responsible for my Mom's happiness. After it ended, she told my Step-Dad that it was ok, and that it was what she envisioned. A day "all about Jennie." This description was said in a tone of disgust. You see, no matter what I did, it wasn't good enough, because it was a happy celebration for me.

My wedding was another day of her drama and was full of crazy stunts! A few months before the wedding date, she decided she wasn't going because I didn't visit her enough. Out of the blue, she sent my Step-Dad over to my house to tell me this news. My Step-Dad was supposed to walk me down the aisle. To share the series of events that led up to this day, I need to take a step back and explain a few things.

My son was now two-years-old and my Mom and Step-Dad never paid much attention to him and barely had any sort of relationship, which was sad as he is such a loving boy who had health difficulties his first few years of life and spent a lot of time in and out of hospitals due to allergies and respiratory issues. When he turned one, we discovered that he had a severe peanut allergy (anaphylaxis) and the doctor warned it could be airborne, and the allergy could be fatal. My parents unfortunately fed the squirrels in their neighborhood whole peanuts and there were peanut shells everywhere outside, including big bulk bags filled with them in their house. I asked my Mom if she could feed the squirrels something else so we could bring my son to visit, which led to another war and comments of "The world revolves around Jennie." They refused to believe me about my son's food allergies and treated it as exaggeration and wanting attention. So, we stopped going over for fear of my son going into anaphylactic shock. My son did have an EpiPen, however an EpiPen does not get rid of an allergic reaction. It's an injection of epinephrine that narrows the blood vessels and opens airways. It "pauses" the allergic reaction for approximately ten minutes, which is why it can literally mean life and death when anaphylaxis hits. 911 needs to be called, and if they aren't there in time, a second EpiPen may be needed to buy you another ten minutes until medical professionals take over.

My Mom didn't believe this allergy and would cause drama all the time about it. She said she tried to accommodate, but then would argue about the squirrels, even buying my son a birthday cake that had peanuts in it. The day of the cake was interesting. You see, she never really took my son's anaphylaxis seriously, plus it was an occasion not about her. In her mind she went through the trouble buying the cake but because I got upset, it made me the selfish one and her efforts unappreciated. My Mom always had a way of making me feel crazy!

Anyways, back to the wedding. When my Step-Dad came to deliver the news as per her instructions, I had nothing to lose and let him have it. I couldn't believe any of it! The fact that she wasn't going to my wedding and was blaming me for not going. Sending my Step-Dad and he was actually fulfilling her orders without question? Did I ever let him have it, finishing my rant with, everyone in their life cannot be wrong. Who is left? She has managed to fight with and alienate everyone in their life. There's no one left. They had alienated everyone, except for my brother and I.

I guess that finally woke him up a little bit (about time!) and he forced my Mom to come over. My Step-Dad, soon to be hubby Gavin and myself, had a talk with her about her behavior. Of course, she viewed this as a full force attack because she could never admit when she was wrong. This was the only time in my Step-Dad's life when he finally stood up to her. I was so hopeful that this would mean our family could be ok moving forward . . . but like I said, this was the only time he ever stood up to her, and it never happened again. After this talk and her being backed into a corner, it was decided they were coming to the wedding. While things calmed down there were still odd behaviors that would pop up, like when my Step-Dad called me to check if it was appropriate for my Mom to wear a white gown to my wedding, that looks like a wedding dress. (Yes, I'm serious but hey, it's baby steps!) While it was great news to have them at my wedding, things turned into a repeat of my baby shower. It became about two things. My Mom and my Mom's need for drama and attention.

She skipped my bridal shower because she was humiliated about the talk between the four of us, because the venue was too far (half an hour away), and I didn't think of her while planning it. Lastly, my Step-Dad's family was invited, so I was accused of taking their side. (Their side in what? They weren't fighting, it was a request to take her side in her hatred and never invite or talk to them ever!). At my wedding, I had to ensure people she didn't like were not seated near her. She did not like that the venue was a half hour away drive away and was upset that my Step-Dad didn't let her wear the "wedding dress." So, they came and I did all I could to avoid her as I really wanted to enjoy my day with my husband and I made the day my dream wedding. It was a big celebration for all to enjoy.

One of my favorite pictures is the dancefloor being full and it is still light out. I captioned it my "Best Day Ever" and it truly was. We found out later that my Mom told our relatives that I used them for my wedding. That I used them as I needed someone to walk me down the aisle and used them for money to pay for the wedding. While we appreciated their gift, it was $1,000. To put this into perspective, it paid for approximately eight people's dinner out of an attendance of 150. I didn't bother going back to all of my relatives to correct her. To me it was our perfect day, and nothing could ruin it. It was the day I became a Mrs. and felt like the luckiest girl on earth!

Narcissistic Personality Disorder (or NPD) is someone who has an exaggerated sense of importance and has a constant need to be the center of attention. They can do no wrong and lack empathy, tend to lie and rewrite history to support their lies, and are pros at gaslighting. Gaslighting is a form of psychological manipulation used to make you question your own memories and sanity. It gives the gaslighter power, because they make their victims feel like they are crazy and had imagined things that actually did happen. Overall, they are generally unhappy and only thrive on drama. Because of this, they rarely have friendships or stable jobs, (it is always the other person's fault, never their own). The tricky part with narcissists is that they don't recognize their flaws and rarely get professional help because they are perfect in their own minds. You see, to a narcissist it is their world and nothing can disrupt their views or their life. They need constant attention, recognition and are very concerned with self-image. The interesting part about NPD, is that underneath is a fragile person that cannot handle any sort of criticism due to lack of self-esteem. NPD moms tend to treat their daughters the worst and use gaslighting as a form of verbal abuse to the point where daughters feel like they are not only not worth loving, but also insane.

Relationships with NPDs are minimal. They have trouble keeping friends, jobs and if they are married or in a relationship, their significant other will either be a narcissist, an enabler or simply absent. Enablers are the most common as they will not challenge any of the negativity or drama and will take a backseat role in the marriage/relationship for fear of rocking the boat. As a father, they will try not to get involved in complicated family dynamics, may even assist in abusing you or might try to ride both sides (i.e., Saying things like, you know how your Mother is ... in other words, you should know better and dismiss the issue). People tend to feel sorry for the enabling fathers as technically they don't do anything bad on their own, but their lack of getting involved also makes them wrong and just as much of an abuser if they are witness to bad behavior. Think of someone witnessing a random crime like a hit and run or where someone gets hurt. If you are watching the accident and don't stop to help, you are just as at fault. Most people would call 911 and step in to help the victim. Or like I mentioned in the bullying chapter, if you witness a bully hurting someone and don't do anything about it, are you in the wrong? YES! In general, they would never have this sort of behavior on their own, but as they are witnessing this behavior they are just as guilty. My Step-Dad fell into the role of an enabler. I wouldn't necessarily say my Step-Dad is a bad person, however, he could have been a better one because there were many times where he could have stepped in and stopped some of the behavior.

There were also times when he would get sucked into the toxic environment and join my Mom in berating me. The extended family and outsiders always felt sorry for him but, looking back, I don't. He was the adult and he could have done so much more.

Narcissistic Mothers fall into two categories.

1. *The Ignoring Mom.* These NPD moms have no interest in their daughter and view her as a nuisance. She will ignore her daughter to the point where basic care gets compromised, but she will take care of her own appearance for the love of compliments. If questioned on her daughter's appearance, she will blame the daughter. In general, she won't get involved in her daughter's interests. She won't go to school events unless it makes her look good and gives her attention. Overall the daughters feel unseen and unwanted. NPD moms will talk about other kids and how well they are doing, implying, why aren't you like them? The daughter will try hard to get attention and please her mom but will most likely fail. One example is; my Aunt would tell my cousin (her daughter) about how successful her dentist's daughters are and then question her own kids as

to why they are not as successful, implying that they are not good enough.

2. *The Engulfing Mom.* These moms are the exact opposite. They want their daughter to be an extension of them and get involved in everything. They have an opinion of everything in her life and have no sense of personal space. They will constantly push their daughters to be better and criticize heavily when they do not live to their expectations. The catch? Expectations can never be met or are good enough in the engulfing mom's eyes.

NPD Moms love tragedies and hate special days for others. They hate special occasions when it's not about them and will do what they can to divert attention to themselves or they try to sabotage. They love when bad things happen to their daughters as they love the drama and will work the situation to ensure they can get some attention and make themselves look good. The better my life got, the worse my Mom got. But when my life was in shambles, my Mom was supportive, to an extent. An example would be when I broke up with a boyfriend. She was there to console me, but then would talk about how she will miss him and remind me that my biological clock is ticking. Then would go back to my Step-Dad to talk about what a mess my life was. Have you ever heard the saying "Misery loves company"?

Take it to the next level and it is called trauma-hijacking. NPDs will take your drama and spin it so they receive the attention they so crave. You see, my Mom was using my trauma to get sympathy from others, especially my Step-Dad, who would then say things like, "You are such a good Mom" and "What are we going to do about that Jennie?" Then I would get it two-fold. I was a mess AND I was putting my Mom out. I would need to thank her repeatedly for being there for me. I would need my Mom for support, but would leave feeling even worse as somehow, I would need to comfort her and apologize for taking her time.

Each time I would visit my Mom, I would leave feeling exhausted. A visit to her would mean insults, gaslighting and most of all walking on eggshells and trying to avoid getting her upset. My Mom could explode for no reason, so you never knew what to expect. These explosions, also called narcissistic rage, are common, happening when an NPD feels threatened as they don't like to be questioned. They see themselves as better than others so do not feel questions are warranted. They get nasty quick, go on the attack and fight dirty. Most times the person on the receiving end, will be surprised at the level of attack, as it seems so unnecessary and exaggerated. But in the mind of an NPD, they are warranted as they can do no wrong. Gaslighting is the other form of abuse that is common. They will insult you but then lie about insulting you and then act like you are crazy for feeling bad about the insult.

There are so many examples when an NPD will make you feel like you're crazy, saying;

- You're too sensitive
- You can't take a joke
- You're so judgmental
- You made me do it
- You always play the victim or always need attention
- You are exaggerating what I said, stop making me be the bad person.

Frequent lines from my childhood were;

- I'm too dramatic, I always need to make my Mom the bad person
- I'm not some princess so my Mom will not treat me that way

- The world does not revolve around me
- The only reason I have friends is that nobody knows the real me but my Mom knows the real me and is still here so I should feel lucky and grateful
- You really are your Dad's daughter (my real Dad who she hated)
- I could help you, but I won't, you shouldn't be so weak. Be independent (age six)

I could write a book on the list of insults, so I'll stop here but the reason I'm listing examples is to help you identify the narcissists in your life. Sometimes when we have these toxic relationships, they hurt you in small subtle ways over time and you may not realize what is happening but have an ongoing sense of something is wrong. Sharing examples may help identify that something is wrong. If you have an NPD in your life, hopefully this will help you acknowledge the relationship and give you the push in deciding whether you can or should tolerate it.

How can you identify if someone has NPD? Honestly, I think us victims always know something is wrong. NPDs just put a name on it. Here are the most popular characteristics of an NPD in the form of a checklist.

- Manipulative—they manipulate the truth to be in control
- Lack empathy—can't recognize others' needs or feelings
- Arrogant—high opinion of themselves, view themselves as better than others
- Entitled—need constant admiration and attention
- Feel powerful, successful, beautiful
- Need to be in control and dominant of others
- Jealous and envious if someone else does better
- Exaggerated sensitivity—cannot take any criticism and will attack if people disagree
- Difficulty maintaining relationships
- Controlling and egotistical
- Always need to be in the spotlight and jealous if not
- Never satisfied
- Making others feel constant guilt for not being good enough
- Temper issues and cutting people out of their life
- Being physically, verbally and/or sexually abusive

I hope this chapter sheds some light on NPDs and maybe even provided some "aha" moments. It's very hard to identify NPDs when you are constantly belittled and put down. Take a second and assess your relationships to ensure that they are healthy. People who care about you lift you up and want you to be happy. Not the opposite.

Chapter 4

Being a Child of Abuse and Its Effects

Can an NPD parent love their children? Narcissists are incapable of love and unfortunately that doesn't change when they have children. A narcissistic parent views their child as a possession and another thing to control for their own agenda. A narcissist's world is very black and white and you are either perfect or trash, with no in between and treated as such. So, as a child, all you want to do is please your parents. You tend to work overtime to ensure that you are perfect. Unfortunately, the perfect standard is unachievable, so the NPD will purposely sabotage their child's confidence using tactics such as guilt, name calling and use the child's insecurities as weapons. It's a matter of making the child small so they stay under the

NPD's control. In other words, no matter what you do, in their eyes you will never be perfect.

The 90 absences in Grade 9 caught the attention of our school counselor who called my mother and I in for a meeting to discuss why I had missed so much school. Unfortunately for me, this counselor had some preconceived notions about teenagers and took her stereotypical views out on me in these sessions. I was skipping school to avoid the bullying or sneaking home to nap because I was exhausted because I was ill. There were times where I had every intention of going to class, but I would see people waiting for me at the door so I would avoid. I tried to share some of the stories about my home life and told her about "bug eyes" and all of the bullying that I had to endure, as well as my overactive thyroid diagnoses but she seemed very focused on me and my "teenage behavior" of skipping school. I can't emphasize how much my Mom loved this counselor! This was another person that would give her sympathy for putting up with me. After one meeting with her, the counselor was convinced that my absences were because I didn't like my Step-dad. My Step-Dad? He had nothing to do with anything! He was an enabler, sure, but never the instigator and not the cause for everything I was experiencing at the age of fourteen!

My Mom loved how it made her look. She would go back to my Step-Dad and tell him all about these sessions. My Mom requested more sessions for me and asked to be included every time. It turned into the Mom show where she did all of the talking and I stopped making an effort to explain my experiences. Instead, the conversations were all about my Mom and everything she does for me and how hard it was for her to raise a daughter like me. Anytime I would talk, my Mom would mock me and tell me I was wrong. We didn't talk about my thyroid, or that I was bullied or even how bad things were at home. One session I walked in with puffy eyes from crying as I just endured another hallway walk of everyone shouting bug eyes and throwing things at me. It went unnoticed. We talked about my Mom and how much she needed my Step-Dad and I need to be respectful of that. Conversations were centered around, what happens when the kids move out of the house, did I want my Mom to be alone? Once again, I became invisible, and honestly too sick and too tired to even attempt taking on my Mom. In her words, the school counselor called her because Jennie was in trouble at school. That Jennie, always in trouble.

Narcissistic Personality Disorder is very difficult to diagnose and only good psychologists can

identify someone with NPD. This counselor unfortunately did not see the full picture in these sessions and could not see past my overbearing Mom
and trusted everything she said at face value. I
wish I had stats to share as to how many psychologists have identified NPDs, however stats are
minimal for this disorder as NDPs rarely get help.
In the initial meeting with the counselor I was
alone, which my Mom did not like and made sure
that she was included in every session following.
These sessions did not help me feel better. It was
just another way to make me feel small and only
made me skip school more to avoid it all together.
When the counselor agreed with my Mom, it
made me question myself. My Mom made me feel
like a terrible person and now a school counselor
is supporting her views. She questioned if I was
exaggerating my bullying to get attention, and
asked if there was anything I had done to provoke
this boy, even once asking if I took this situation
wrong, insinuating that it didn't happen.

Even when I was doing well, my Mom turned
it around on me. There were a few teachers over
the years, who called my Mom to compliment my
writing and presentation skills and told her that I
was gifted and could have a future in literary arts if
I kept working on it. When she talked to me about

it, she would question their education and state they didn't know what they were talking about. In Grade 5, we had monthly presentations. Students would pick a topic and then write an essay to read to the class. My teacher was so impressed with one of my essays that she couldn't wait to see what came next and offered to tutor me after class hours. She called my Mom again to tell her I could have a future in writing. My Mom, seeing that I was getting attention, criticized my writing so much that I lost my confidence and passion. I gave up. I didn't care how my next essay turned out because I didn't want to fight with my Mom anymore. The next month I received a failing grade. Obviously, this confused the teacher as to how I could go from an A+ grade to an F in a matter of a month. So, yet another phone conversation. Sharing her concern, my Mom responded with an "I told you so." She repeated that I am not a writer, maybe I copied someone's work the month prior, it sounds like something I would do. Writing is something that I have always been self-conscious about because of the attention I did receive in school and the berating I received from my Mom. I still find it ironic that I am now writing a book.

As I got older and started meeting and learning about other families, I realized normal family units do not operate this way. They want their children to succeed, to be happy and they support their children. Working in retail and in the restaurant industry (increasing my "bubbles"), I would meet so many different types of people, and I noticed that the majority all had one thing in common. Their parents and families loved them and supported them. They enjoyed family celebrations and couldn't wait until Thanksgiving. It was so strange to me, as my life was spent looking at a calendar and dreading any sort of family get together because they would always end in a fight. My Mom would make any get together a drama filled one for various reasons, usually because I didn't put enough thought into things, or did something else wrong.

I became more observant of other families and tried to remove my fear of not being wanted from clouding my judgment, to see if my Mom could be the problem. Removing this fear was so difficult. Sometimes trying to remove yourself from the situation helps give perspective. If you imagine you were giving advice to a friend, it can be eye opening. Having spent my life of trying to hide my Moms behavior from friends, I realized I was not only hiding things from other people, I was hiding a lot from myself. Writing this book, memories were coming back that I had entirely removed from my mind. I had been suppressing things from my memory. As I grew older, I did try to tell my family how I felt, but my Mom would view these conversations as an attack on her, so I would back off immediately. I once tried to talk to my Step-Dad, but all that did was get back to my Mom and same result... attack! So, I started to read, and read, and read. I tried to find any answers out there. I still didn't fully trust professional help given my experiences as a child, so I went to where I could trust. Books!

I always trusted books as they were my way of escape as a child, plus I have this uncanny talent of being able to read an entire book in a day. I started researching mother and daughter relationships and tried to find subjects to which I could relate. The closest thing that I had found was maybe my Mom had a version of Munchausen syndrome by proxy. Munchausen syndrome by proxy is a type of mental illness in which the caregiver will physically harm their child, change test results, or lie about their child's symptoms to take the child to a healthcare professional and receive attention or sympathy. From the outside, the caregiver looks devoted for taking care of her ill child while on the inside they are harming their child on purpose for the sake of getting attention. I didn't think she had Munchausen in a physical sense, but I was curious if there was a verbal version of this.

My Mom was only happy when I was unhappy. Any time I was happy or getting attention, she would do all she could to sabotage that happiness or make me feel guilty or stupid for believing in the happiness. She loved when things were not going well for me and thrived when I was sad. This meant she could play the role of a supportive Mom and get recognition from outsiders and my Step-Dad, when in reality she was usually the cause for when things weren't going well in my life. I saw similarities with Munchausen, messing with the child's physical health for attention. I felt my Mom was messing with my mental health to get attention. So many examples came to mind where I realized that she would always sabotage anything good that came my way but, was so supportive and happy when my life was in shambles. It sounded so crazy to me, but I could relate to it 100%. Finally, I felt like I was on to something and I kept looking for books, desperate for knowledge because I knew I didn't want to accept this as normal anymore and I wanted answers. I especially didn't want my kids to experience anything that I went through. Then the day came when I figured out what was wrong, and my life changed. I believe my Mom has Narcissistic Personality Disorder.

I only discovered this because my cousin had found information that outlined this disorder and brought it to my attention. My Mom has a sister who shows similar characteristics and she has two daughters. These two daughters had some similar experiences in their childhood. Our Moms had sabotaged our relationship early in life, so we never had the opportunity to compare stories or be there for each other. We only reconnected as adults and shared our experiences, realizing how our childhoods were unhealthy. We all recognized that something was wrong, but it was so complicated and crazy. Plus, we were reduced to being so insecure and sometimes depressed that it was hard to shake the shame and the guilt to look for and accept answers. When my cousin sent me this information, it changed everything. In all my reading, I didn't come across any information on it. It explained my upbringing and for the first time I understood who my parents were and why I was treated the way I was.

Abuse can be obvious and in your face, too subtle and hard to distinguish. Sometimes victims may not realize they are abused and some people may not understand the subtle abuses. The way I was treated was consistent all my life so I didn't know any better and thought it was normal. My abuse could be classified as emotional (verbally undermining an individual's self-worth), to psychological (intimidation, isolation, threats). Other abuses can can be categorized as physical (hitting or any type hurt imposed by touch), sexual (without consent), and economic (total control over finances leaving the person trapped).

The effects of abuse on a person can be long lasting and may include some of these characteristics;

1. *Self-blame*—The victim tends to blame themselves and believes if I change myself, I'll be loved. Maybe if I'm quieter, maybe if I'm happier etc. When it comes to NPD moms and their children, this gets heightened as kids tend to hide their real feelings being fearful of confrontation. The Mom will typically follow with more insults and further verbally abuse their child. For me, I felt self-blame because "The world always had to revolve around Jennie."

2. *Echoism*—is looking to please, and it can be exhausting. We simply "echo" our abuser's thoughts and sayings. With children, all they want is for their parents to be proud and they try to make their mom happy.

When my Mom disliked someone, I would act like I did to, in hopes that she would praise me.

3. *Insecure attachment*—is looking for a life vest or safety net. You run to be attached to someone as you feel there is no stability. Being thrown out of my house all the time, caused me to get into relationships looking for a "home." You chase love, make up love, anything for some form of stability. I used to wish for a home as I always felt lost. My dream when I was eight was owning my own apartment and eating Viva Puffs! The basics of food and shelter. The ongoing neglect and abuse make you feel unwanted and amplifies the need of finding someone who wants you.

4. *Need-panic*—Making the victim scared to ask for their needs so they don't, unless they can't avoid asking for a need which then leads to panic. My Mom would call this—teaching me to be independent. When I got my first period, I couldn't avoid asking for help and I didn't fully understand what was going on (I heard girls talk about it here and there, but my Mom never fully explained it to me). I dreaded asking for

help as I knew I would get in trouble. I was so scared to tell her! Giving the news of my period caused a battle as she had had a long day and now, she had to go out and get pads, which caused me to burst into tears. Her response was typical, "Ohhh, poor Jennie always make me out to be the bad guy, just because Jennie gets her period doesn't mean the world stops."

5. *Independence*—sounds like a positive word and something we all strive for, however when abused you learn that you can only depend on yourself from an early age. You have a fear to need anything, so you become self-reliant. My Mom would say she was "teaching me to be independent" to not support me or as an excuse to neglect my needs.

When it comes to being raised by an NPD, children can have life-long self-esteem issues, lack of confidence, trust issues, prone to addictions, self-harm and self-neglect. They may also never figure out who they truly are as they are used to constantly trying to please someone and getting criticized and verbally abused. They experience a disconnect between their feelings and reality and are paranoid about people being upset at them. Anxiety is very common as they are constantly second guessing themselves. Feelings of worthlessness can lead to thoughts of suicide. They dream of being rescued from their life, hoping things will change on its own because they feel they have no control in their life. They expect people to deliberately want to cause harm. And they look to fill the void. A career, or marriage can function as a band-aid, a distraction from looking at their true self. I remember I once had a boss that said to me, "Nobody is out to get you or wants you to fail." And I thought to myself, they don't?

It's a tricky balancing act, as they are craving recognition and attention yet are concerned about being selfish. I still need to remind myself, that I am not being selfish, and it is ok to be happy and proud of your accomplishments. It takes a while to retrain your thinking and be able to recognize what you have been through. Acknowledging is the first step to healing.

Children of NPDs can fall into two classes;

1. *Underachiever*—An Underachiever will try to self-sabotage, make excuses for never succeeding and not have the drive to try to improve their life. They feel that their tough life is a reason to not strive for more. They

use their upbringing as a crutch for everything wrong that happens in their life.

2. *Overachiever*—An Overachiever feels the never-ending quest to feel good about themselves and yet nothing will ever feel good enough. They constantly push themselves to be more or do more for acknowledgment and praise. Praise is their motivator and they are starving for it as they received little to none.

I was an Overachiever to the point of exhaustion, and it was not healthy. I was so desperate to prove my Mom wrong that I was not the terrible person she made me feel like I was. Only her words never disappeared no matter how hard I worked or how successful I became. A Mom's words are powerful and hard to erase.

Being an overachiever was great for my career as it has always been evolving. However, this also means being in constant need of recognition for fear of never doing enough. Through high school I often had 2–3 jobs at the same time and worked a lot of hours. I used work as an escape because my Mom would never argue if I was going to work. The need for approval also gave me the drive to work hard. Starting to work when I was young, taught me life skills, gave me a sense of independence and gave me the approvals and acceptance that I had been looking for. I found it easier to talk to people at work as you could stick to safe subjects like small talk or talk about work, avoiding talk of my home life entirely. Because of this I was able to make friends easier. Nobody I worked with cared about my family life or saw any of the weirdness I experienced at home. My first job at a fast food restaurant helped me find friendships and my first real long-term relationship boyfriend. And for the first time in my life, taught me confidence and some sense of security. Also, it made me feel like maybe I'm not a freak and a terrible person! I viewed working hard as a way to plan my future, a future away from my Mom. Even to the present day, I'm working at Mattel in a unique dual role that was created just for me. I still have the need for acceptance and approval but not to the extent of when I was younger. Now my need for acceptance has evolved to a need of feeling proud of what I'm doing. It's a healthier spin on what drives me.

Mattel was the first job I had where they let me be me. They created and tailored my roles which made me realize that being different is ok. One of my career highlights that brought my life full circle was meeting Erica Ehm! As a child

I would watch her on MuchMusic as a VJ, interviewing the coolest people in music. Being super awkward, shy and feeling out of place, I would watch Erica Ehm and think to myself, how can someone be so cool and sure of themselves? I would watch her almost every day and wish to be as cool as her. This year I met her and I was star struck. Meeting Erica Ehm who was a childhood idol, represented to me that maybe I am good! If I could be at the same event as her, I must be doing all right. We took a selfie together with my daughter (Erica taught me how to do proper selfies with timers!). Seems like a little thing but if I could tell kid-Jennie that when she grows up, she'll be at the CN Tower for a Barbie party with Erica Ehm, she would have never believed it! It was one of those moments that brought me back to my complicated childhood and made me appreciate how far I have come.

My Mom didn't want me getting a secondary education. After high school I took a year off to try and decide what I wanted to do with my life. With no direction it was easy to not want anything out of my life. Easy to accept being a failure as it seemed like that's all my Mom wanted for me. I thought that the best thing to do was just work and save my money to get out of my parents' house. While I worked hard in High School, I didn't save any money. I was bringing in paychecks of $200–$300 bi-weekly but my Mom was taking a large portion. She would split my paychecks into thirds. One third she would take for rent. One third she would put into a savings account for me (I never saw this money again). And one third I could keep, however, now I had to buy my own groceries and clothes. I was falling behind financially, because she used to buy my clothes and food. One third of $200–$300 equaled approx. $5–$7/day. I was barely getting by on many meals of Spaghettios and fast food using my employee discount.

After high school the only thing that kept nagging at me was that I would love to be able to help people but had no idea how. I started looking for camp counseling jobs and secured one with the City of Etobicoke and it was awesome! I finally felt like I was making a difference, however minimal, and I loved it! After that summer, I got my first full time day job at Levi's working in a store and slowly worked my way up to Assistant Manager. I worked nights at a pub as a hostess and then went on to waitressing/bartending. I worked every hour possible, which obviously strained things with my high school boyfriend Peter as we didn't have a lot of time together because he went right to college after high school. He knew that my parents didn't encourage education and was insistent on bettering myself and trying school. I give him a lot of credit for getting me started on a better path. Whenever I mentioned school, my Mom thought my job at the pub was good enough and said "I'm just looking for ways to piss away money." Bartending/serving is great, but I wasn't passionate about it. I knew I wanted to do something different and I always had dreams of somehow helping people and wanting to do more. Without Peter's encouragement and drive I don't think I would have saved all of my restaurant money to pay for college or buy my first car. He always saw my potential and pushed me to be more.

So, I worked my two jobs, saved all my money, bought my first car and went to college, fighting with my Mom every step of the way. She would say "I don't want that thing (car) in my driveway," "What's the point of college you already make good money," "There's no way that you'll make more money than you do now" or my favorite, "What? You think you're better than me?" (My Mom didn't go to college), "I don't like your college. People that go there think they're better than people like us. It's a bad college. I don't like that Peter is making you do this. If he asked you to jump off a bridge would you?" It was around this time that Peter and I started wondering if my Mom was jealous of me. There was something wrong with this behavior. Most parents would be ecstatic that their daughter worked hard and bought a car and paid for school on her own. Most parents want their kids to be happy and successful. Not my Mom!

I have come to the realization that my Mom's behavior was abusive, and I was not brought up in a normal family environment. I still worry about new people and if they are pretending to like me. Sometimes I replay conversations in my head to assess if I was too much (too braggy, too happy, too much emotion) but not to the extent of my childhood. I am comfortable with my tight-knit circle of friends and family that I keep close.

Since writing this book, I realized I underestimated the impact on me and it made me assess relationships and clean out the remaining narcissists in my life. I'm not sure if the road for healing will ever end, but knowledge is power. Realizing that some quirks or sensitivities are normal for someone who has been through these experiences, gives me acceptance. If you think you were abused, do try to get to the cause and identify what kind of abuse you experienced. Start researching and you'll see that you are not alone. You can get help, everyone is deserving of love. I encourage you to start looking into how to rebuild and find where you fit. Look deep in yourself and identify what are your triggers, acknowledge what wounds still need mending and what are your needs to help you get to a place of forgiveness and get you to your path to happiness!

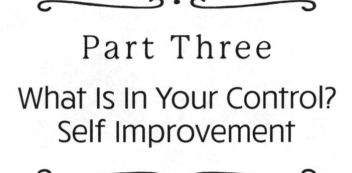

Part Three

What Is In Your Control?
Self Improvement

Chapter 5

Power of Thought

My family life didn't make me a believer in spirituality or religion. As a child, I would have darker thoughts and wish to run away and escape my life. In my early teens, I thought about ending my life entirely and did not feel loved or wanted by anyone. I was taught to remain small and unseen and anytime I shone, it was mocked, reduced to nothing or I was accused of always needing to be the center of attention. I was comfortable being a victim thinking "shit always happens to me," using it as a reason not to try and have a better life. I went through the motions of being "normal," putting on a happy face, saying things I thought people wanted to hear, but really, I was suffering inside. Accepting being the victim and not feeling any

self-worth, I didn't realize that my thought process could be further complicating my life and
making it worse. I complained about boys, lack of
finances and focused on the miserable upbringing
that I had. I wasn't open to any advice or solutions
to change my life because I didn't believe it could
be changed. Feeling unloved by your own mother
is probably the worst feeling a human can feel.
If my own mom doesn't love me, then I must be
unlovable and not worth love.

In Grade 9/10 while being bullied severely at
school for my "bug eye" appearance, I was also
being treated poorly at home. My Mom would
accuse me of exaggerating how I felt or making things up for attention. On the really bad
days, I was threatened with being kicked out of
the house because she couldn't take it anymore
(which she actually did throw me out later on and
did it numerous times). I was on about 10 pills a
day. I was constantly sick and could barely function. I was tired and going to bed after school from
sheer exhaustion, then waking up the next morning to start my day all over again. Every morning
as I walked to the bus stop, I would throw up on
the same two front lawns from the medication I
was on. (Those poor people, years later I dropped
off flowers anonymously on their doorstep.) I was

seeing a thyroid specialist weekly who would monitor my heart rate and thyroid levels and adjust my prescriptions accordingly. The drives to this specialist were terrible as my Mom would just lay on the guilt of how much time I was taking out of her busy life and that I better not be exaggerating my symptoms. This was laughable as my blood tests proved how sick I was.

Every week the appointment would follow the same routine. My Mom acting like the hero, getting sympathy and advice from the doctor, and me sitting in the room like I was invisible. The doctor was a great enabler for my Mom as she loved the attention and loved being praised for taking care of me (You can see the synergies with Munchausen, right?). When we started these weekly appointments, I would ask questions as it was pretty scary what was happening to me and I didn't fully understand my illness. Anytime I would ask a question, my Mom would laugh and say some sort of comment that would make me feel stupid. "Jennie, we talked about this at home and the doctor is busy."

My Mom never sat me down to explain my thyroid. I started thinking, well maybe this is when I die and that's ok because nobody wants me. The only way I could learn about my thyroid is by secretly going to the library to read about it. This brought on a new level of fear as the books would say that if the medication does not work, then removing half my thyroid would be the only option. Removal comes with a new set of problems. If they remove too much, it turns underactive and lifelong maintenance is needed. Somewhere down the line, I gave up in these appointments in fear of being ridiculed and didn't want to feel stupid for not understanding. I stopped asking questions, stopped caring about what was happening to me and as usual tried to make myself small and unnoticeable and let the doctor and my Mom talk about me like I wasn't even there.

After about a year of this, the doctor's treatment plan was still not working. Each week the doctor would either increase my medication (which would make me more sick) or tell me to be patient and that it would work if we just kept at it. The doctor was starting to talk about removing half of my thyroid as his treatment wasn't showing any progress. Having already done my own reading, this option terrified me. When removing half of your thyroid, the hope is that your thyroid levels would balance out. Unfortunately, it's quite common for your thyroid to become underactive which is not curable.

Your body slows down, with slower metabolism making you tired all the time.

Two events led to my breaking point. The first was when I was doing laundry and pulling my clothes out of the dryer. All of my clothes were covered in so much of my hair that you could barely tell what color they were. I remember crying as I pulled my clothes out of the dryer and kept trying to pull hair off, but no matter how much I tried there was just too much hair. My Mom of course minimized how depressed I was and ridiculed how I reacted to this. She called me dramatic and just yelled at me to clean up the mess of hair, threatening that if I broke the dryer, I had to buy the family a new one. I gave up on the clothes and couldn't stop staring in the mirror, hating my reflection as I too thought I was a bug eye freak. I would measure my bald spots, try to push my gouging eyes back into my eye sockets so they wouldn't stick out so much. I just hated myself.

The second event happened weeks later. I woke up at 7 and took my morning dosage of pills, got dressed in my school uniform and went upstairs. I lived in our basement at this time. I loved it down there as I could hide and be out of sight, out of mind. I saw my Mom who asked why I was still in my uniform? I said it was 7, so I had to leave soon to get to school. She laughed and said it's 7 p.m. not 7 a.m. and ridiculed my stupidity. I then panicked and told her that I already took my morning dosage of pills. I was on such a big dosage that it could compromise my heart, health, and I could OD. Now the details of this date are a bit hazy, I can't remember if she took me to the doctor or called the doctor. But I ended up being ok health wise and was instructed to carry on my pill dosages.

The dryer experience and the risk of an overdose made such an impact on me and was the turning point. I honestly didn't care what happened to me, I just knew that I didn't want to live like this anymore. Imagine living your life in a fog, tired all the time and on top of it, ridiculed and made to feel guilty about being sick? Constantly feeling like a zombie, bullied at school, and nauseous all the time. It pushed me to my breaking point. Something just snapped in me and it's hard to explain but I found new strength, and it was a little unsettling. I knew I didn't want to live like this and took some major risks with my wellbeing. I changed the way I thought about my life, I wanted to live a healthy one.

From that day onward, every morning at 7 a.m. I went into the bathroom and flushed my pills down the toilet. Every morning I looked in the mirror and said to myself, I am no longer going to live like this, and I am going to get better on my own. Every week I went to my specialist appointments and didn't say a word. Not that I said much prior to this moment anyway, so my silence wasn't noticed. Then slowly, I started noticing changes. Small at first, but I noticed my hair was starting to grow back. Where I once had bald spots, little new baby hairs were growing (They didn't help my appearance but showed that my health was changing). Then one morning, I walked to the school bus and didn't throw up on anyone's front lawns. I slowly started thinking clearly, wasn't exhausted and hot and sweaty all the time. Somehow, I started feeling normal! Slowly but surely every week the doctor reported back, that my thyroid levels had decreased. Every morning I never wavered, I didn't take another pill again. I kept wishing to be healthy, speaking to myself in the mirror telling myself I don't need these pills. All the while, keeping my love for flushing pills down the toilet a secret.

A few months later, my reoccurring appointments had been reduced as I was no longer a severe case. My Mom did not like this and questioned the doctor, but my health was no longer at a level where these appointments were warranted.

I found this humorous as she used to yell at me about the number of times we had to go to the doctor. She questioned his competence, calling him an idiot behind his back. Then finally the day I had been dreaming about arrived. My doctor gave me the news that I had been praying and hoping for. My thyroid levels were normal. His "treatment plan" was working and he didn't think I needed surgery anymore. I was in shock and wondered if this was all too good to be true but, I could tell a difference in how I was feeling and my appearance was almost normal, so it was possible. I kept quiet while my Mom and the doctor congratulated themselves on their hard work. The interesting part is that the doctor still wanted me to be on my pills, reducing them slowly, which was fine with me as I wasn't taking them anyway, so I continued to pretend and flushed my pills down the toilet. I continued to talk to myself to my reflection in the mirror every morning, willing myself to get better.

The day finally came when I broke the news. This charade had been going on long enough. I told the truth. I hadn't been taking my pills for a few months. Well let me tell you, everyone lost it on me. To be fair, they had every right to. I knew I was playing a dangerous game with my health. I was whisked away for so many tests, as they feared for my heart and other health issues. The doctor was upset with me for not consulting him. My Mom freaked out as I didn't tell her, so I made her look like a fool. She complained to the Doctor, "You see what I have to deal with?" But all of the tests came back . . . CLEAR! I never had an issue with my thyroid again!*

I can't help but think that getting healthy was not a coincidence. That my thought process had changed and the act of going into the bathroom every morning and every night to talk to myself in the mirror and tell myself that I'm going to get better, is what changed my health and my life. I had the courage and determination to get better. And I did!

The worst break-up of my life is another experience that forced me to stop, change my thinking and improve myself. I was so in love with Joe and at the time thought he was it and we were going to get married. Joe and I worked together at a CPG (Consumer Packaged Goods) company. He was five years younger than me and I knew he had a crush on me for a long time. I always

---

* Disclaimer, I am not a health professional and am not recommending anyone to go against a doctor's orders and not take medication. I am only telling this story to share my interpretation on the strength of the power of thought.

ignored it, thought he was a nice guy and all but thought the age difference and maturity gap was too wide. Joe was over six feet tall, with brown spiky hair, not the most attractive boyfriend I had had, but a big guy with an even bigger personality. He would exaggerate the truth often, was a chain smoker, a hard drinker, a world traveler and 100% self-destructive. Totally perfect for my self-destructive ways, right? We ended up getting together after a crazy night of partying and were inseparable since. There was a huge maturity gap. He still lived with his wealthy parents in their huge house where his mom still did his shopping and laundry. Whereas I lived on my own, renting an apartment with zero support from anyone. Eventually he unofficially moved in and never officially contributed to the household bills. Our relationship was irresponsible, full of excitement, travel, partying and passion. This was a great example of losing my identity and I couldn't get enough.

The self-destructive trait was something we had in common but we came from completely different backgrounds. His family was wealthy, had family dinner every Sunday, had family rituals of pumpkin picking and tree picking every year. I loved his mom, she was someone I used to dream of what a mom should be. Some of her rituals I still carry on to this day with my own family. Not surprisingly, his family questioned my family background and how it would impact him, worried about me being a bad influence on their son. I found this extremely funny, as I was usually the one trying to keep him out of trouble. Many times I would need to step-in so he didn't get into a fist fight, not max out his credit card at the casino, have to talk him out of buying the entire bar a round of shots, or not to street race the guy that looked "douchey" next to us. Joe never needed to grow up. If his credit card was maxed out, his dad would pay for it. His parents bought him suits for work, did his laundry, made his dentist appointments, would buy his cars and take care of the maintenance. In some ways, he was an adventurer and in other ways he was a child. His safety net contributed to his self-destruction as he never had any repercussions (I'm actually surprised he never ended up in jail! Or maybe he did? Who knows?). I see now that he wasn't a bad person, just spoiled and immature. Failures make you learn the big life lessons, and his failures were covered up and taken care of by the family who supported him in everything. He wanted his life to be exciting, even lying to people about being in the war. He was worried people would learn his secret. He was a spoiled rich kid who lived with his parents in their big mansion.

The "big" break-up as I call it, happened in May and let me tell you, it was the best thing that could have happened to me as it started a series of events that turned my life into what it is today. It's almost as if my life was waiting for this break-up, so it could begin. This relationship needed to be demolished. Sometimes things in your life need to be destroyed to make room for your next step. We had returned from a one-week cruise with some friends where he drank way too much and gambled a lot and he lost so much money that his credit card was being declined. He was upset, as his dad paid his credit card bills. He was worried about how mad his dad was going to be. It was typical of Joe to pick fights with me whenever he was grumpy, so I was used to it and didn't think anything of it when he started picking fights with me the moment we got to the airport and continued the entire way home. His dad picked us up at the airport, and I assumed he was dropping us off at my apartment. However, that night Joe went home saying he wanted to unpack. It didn't bother me as he could be moody and would usually snap out of these moods after he put himself on a "time out."

The next day, he showed up at my apartment looking somber and broke up with me, out of the blue without warning and without reason other than saying "It's not working." I was shocked! After that, I never heard from him again, other than a text asking when he could get his stuff from my apartment. After spending almost every day together for two years, it was like he died as he literally disappeared. It was so drastic! I had such a tough time because there was no time to process that anything was wrong. His family reached out to express their shock and dismay and were downright mad at him. They told me there were a few family battles about it, as they felt like he was making a huge mistake. I would talk to them because it was the only thing keeping him in my life in some form, plus I had grown close to them. I loosely kept in touch with mutual friends, but it was hard. I was such a mess from this "death" that eventually those friendships faded away. I had made my world about his, so losing those friendships hurt and amplified the loneliness.

I went from expecting a ring any day, to him disappearing out of my life entirely. While I was used to losing people in my life, I was not used to losing someone so unexpectedly. I felt like he died, and his friends and family weren't consoling me.

I was losing them as well. My world evaporated. It brought back so many buried insecurities and old issues of abandonment. How could someone just disappear out of your life like that? I had been through break-ups before, but there was still some contact or weakness when an ex would reach out or send a drunk text. There were signs leading to a break-up so it was a little expected and not shocking. I felt discarded and worthless and literally at rock bottom.

I was on a roller coaster of emotions and while this break-up was the worst one I had ever experienced, a funny thing happened. I went from feeling the lowest of the low, never wanting to get out of bed, drinking too much, calling in sick to work, just lacking the energy to live, to opening my eyes and finally seeing some clarity. My life and this breakup was not about him, it was about me and I didn't want to live like this anymore. Why do these things keep happening to me? The answer . . . ME! It made me realize, that I'm accountable for me. Why did I have a series of dead-end relationships? Why did I accept being treated poorly? Why did I keep dating the same type of self-destructing men? These questions led to the same answer. ME!

This was my biggest "Aha" moment and gave me courage to wish for more. I truly believe that everything happens for a reason and I believe that Joe came into my life because I needed a big wake-up call. At thirty-three years old, I was single, on my own, had no plan but something changed in my life. I now had hope and was determined to change my patterns. My life needed to be demolished to make way for my new path. I needed to learn who I am, who my friends are and what I wanted out of my life.

That same summer, I also lost my best friend. People show their true colors when you need to depend on them. The day Joe broke up with me, I went to my best friend's condo. I really needed someone to talk to as I was devastated and couldn't envision how to move on. I couldn't stop crying, and I was hyperventilating a few times throughout the day. While at her condo, she kept trying to pressure me to go to a nightclub with a bunch of our friends. She actually got mad at me when I said I couldn't. I mean, my life just fell apart! I ended up driving home and didn't talk to her for months. In a matter of one day, I lost two very important people in my life. And thank goodness I did!

While starting over was tough, I developed some of the strongest friendships I've ever had and did what I wanted to do for the first time. I read a lot and worked on myself. I spent time with people who cared about me and I got to know myself for the first time. Don't get me wrong, I had good days and bad days, it was a roller coaster of emotions. Some days I made checklists of goals and others, I went to a bar, drank too many shots and drunk dialed my ex. Slowly the bad days became less, and I felt like there was this tiny voice inside me saying this was supposed to happen. It gave me strength to keep moving and start treating myself better. I still had weak days, trying to reach Joe (who never answered), or trying to forgive my best friend (she was of no support), but for the most part, I got to know myself and you know what? I started liking myself! Never in my thirty-three years had I ever thought that I might be a good person! For the first time in my life, I wished for a husband and family. Before, I never felt like I deserved them.

That summer I would wish for these things daily! I gave up hope on having kids in my early twenties because a doctor told me that the chances were minimal due to having endometriosis. But for some reason that summer gave me the courage to wish and dream for a life that I truly wanted. My thought process evolved. I remember saying to my Mom, I'm glad this all happened to me as I'm happy! She was surprised and tried to remind me of my biological clock and the fact that I'm alone and reminded me that I can't move back home. My Mom was great(ish) to me when I was miserable, as if she enjoyed it when my life wasn't going well. So, during this time, she was there for me. It was when my life was going well that she turned into a nightmare. She loved that I was going through a rough time and would talk to my Step-Dad about what a mess I was at thirty-three, "What are we going to do with that Jennie?"

I later learned that Joe cheated on me with another girl he worked with and that was the reason for the out of the blue breakup. She worked at the same company and knew about me and I had known her. There was no girl code on this one. Joe ended up marrying her a few years later. When I heard the news, something surprising happened. I didn't care! Ironically enough, I heard that she cheated on him and they are divorced now. She ended up marrying the guy with whom she cheated. While I never thought karma was a thing . . . WOW! That was karma if I ever did see it!

The experience forced me to do the scariest thing imaginable . . . want more out of my life, be accountable for my life and dream big! Everything happens for a reason and sometimes you need to destroy to rebuild. I think my world needed to be destroyed for me to be ready for my next chapter. That summer was hard but got me ready for a better life. It made me think about the "why," learn to rebuild and most importantly, dream for a better life! One without people who treated me poorly. One with happiness. And one with a husband and family. The biggest shift was my thought process. Before this summer, I thought I didn't deserve a good life and it was mirrored in the boys I dated. I believed there was something wrong with me, because my own mom didn't love me. I continued my dating patterns fueled by a desire to make a home. But I wasn't searching for a home in any of the right places. People treated me the way I let them, and it was a reflection of how I treated myself.

A lot of people say everything happens for a reason as a way of explaining bad experiences, and to give reassurance. Growing up I thought this saying was bullshit. I could not understand why bad things kept happening to me. Now I fully believe that everything does happen for a reason and that life does contain that little piece of magic that can't be rationally explained. While I do believe there are also accidents, I also believe that we put into motion things in our life by our power of thought and that if certain things are meant to be, they will happen. This break-up forced me to assess my life and led me on the road to the love of my life. It was the start of my happily ever after. Little did I know that five months later I would meet my husband, Gavin!

That summer while having wine with a girl-friend, she encouraged me to set up an online dating profile. I was going out a lot and meeting men, but no one really interested me. I don't think there was anything wrong with the men that I was meeting, but with my newfound look on life I wanted to make sure I knew what I was looking for in a partner and worried that I would meet the same guy in my old patterns. So, when the topic of an online profile came up I thought, why not? With my new way of thinking and trying new things, I thought what could go wrong? I took a chance and set up a very realistic profile, no covering up or elaborating the truth. I met two men, Gavin being the second. We went to a restaurant and stayed for about five hours of nonstop talking and laughing. After this date, I ignored my online profile, then canceled it. With Gavin, there were no uncomfortable silences. It was like we had known each other for a long time and were old friends.

My first impression of Gavin can be summarized in one word, Happy. He had a huge smile with these dimples, I couldn't stop staring. I found him very attractive with his dark hair, blue eyes and yes, those dimples, but there was something more and that's where the word happy comes into play. He had this aura about him that exuded happiness, appreciativeness and contentment. He was so polite, genuine, nice to the servers, opened doors and was such a gentleman. He had a funny sense of humor and would laugh at his own jokes, which I liked as it instantly made me laugh as well (He had the Dad jokes perfected before becoming a Dad). It's hard to describe the feelings I had on that date as there were so many. I was in awe of someone who could be so happy, especially since it's something I've been searching for my whole life. I knew then that he was someone I wanted and needed. He was someone special.

My second date with him was a little over a week later. This meant a week of trying to play it cool. Gavin showed me his new house. He had just taken possession. It was empty without any furniture, but he wanted to meet at his house because he was proud of his first home. The date wasn't anything fancy. We were so comfortable around each other, that spending time together was all that was needed. I offered to help him clean the house. May not be thought of as romantic, but any time spent with Gavin was fun, even while cleaning rugs and walls. Our relationship grew and I was at his house all weekend, and every weekend up to the day he used the "L" word for the first time. The "love" word took me a while to return, but not because of him. Even though I had come so far, I still had that fear of people leaving and had a fear of jumping into something so serious so soon based on my destructive relationship patterns. I didn't last long though, and when I did say it, it was awkwardly blurted out while we were watching TV. Embarrassing but also typical of me.

Now, here is the amazing part to reinforce that there is magic in life and the power of positive thought is real. As I was getting my life together, Gavin was too. Unbeknownst to me, Gavin was buying a house after years of renting apartments. When he bought his house, he told his Mom that he wished to soon fill his house with a family. My summer of rebuilding and wishing for a family was similar to his, because he too was ready to settle down. Exactly a year (to the day) after Gavin moved into his house, we had a son and were soon to be married. Within 3.5 years I had a husband, a son, and was pregnant with my daughter. Now my son is eight, and my daughter is six, and Gavin and I have been happily married for almost seven years. Had I met him earlier in my life, we probably wouldn't have connected. I was still on my self-destructive journey and he was in a different place in his life. This all happened when I started wanting more for my life and got the courage to wish for happiness.

While we were so happy to be having a baby, there was a lot of adjusting and planning in such a short period of time. Gavin and I had already exchanged the love word and were committed to each other, but we were still early in our relationship. We lived about an hour apart and prior to the pregnancy, we would mostly see each other on weekends, with the odd dinner mid-week when we would meet halfway. I can't remember the exact day when I started to feel different, but I know I had really bad nausea that kept getting worse. I was light-headed often and I was tired all the time. It wasn't until one day at work, I was at the Toys-R-Us head office watching a presentation about their annual plan which included many pictures of babies. Seeing all the cute babies on screen got me thinking, is this why I'm not feeling well? It started an inner dialogue/argument in my head. Could I be pregnant? There was no way with my endometriosis. The symptoms matched those of pregnancy, but there is no way ... or is there? I didn't really take the thought seriously as I remember what the doctor told me all those years ago, but just in case, I drove to a drugstore after the meeting to get a pregnancy test. I drove right to my apartment and took the test. Well, to say I was shocked is an understatement. I couldn't believe it when I saw it was positive.

At first, I thought that I would wait until the weekend when I was planning on spending time with Gavin at his house, but how can anyone sit on news like this? I was freaking out! And to be truthful, there was this feeling of overwhelming excitement! I knew that things were going to be tough and messy, but OMG could I really be pregnant? The plan of waiting to talk face to face, well, that plan lasted 5 minutes and I ended up calling him and blurting it out over the telephone. His reaction was so calming. He wasn't freaking out, he was. . . . happy! No questions, no doubt, no worries. I knew 100% I wanted this baby however, I was still freaked out and didn't think that he fully understood what this meant. So, I told him to take the night to process this information and we would talk in the morning. I wanted to see how he would feel once he fully digested the news. The next morning, I woke up to a text message from him. All it said was, "I'm so happy!"

His reaction was the best, and never did he falter. Now we had to start talking about life decisions and prepare. The romance continued while we figured things out, bought our first house together (his house was over an hour away and too far for my commuting to work), worked hard and prepared for our little miracle. In just over a year, I went from being single to having a boyfriend, a house and a son! We had created a home, my first true home where I felt loved and wanted. The house wasn't anything special, in fact we had people thinking we were crazy for buying it as it was a true fixer upper and very small. It had a hair salon on the main level and different colored floors, but we loved it and created so many loving memories there. One of my favorites is waiting outside with my son while on mat leave and greeting Gavin when he got home from work. Something so simple.

So how could our lives have changed so much in one year? Was it that our thought patterns had changed? Was it that we both wished hard enough to have a family? Was it that we were meant to meet when we did and were ready for each other, and then everything fell into place?

All these events had to happen in order to get us to where we were when we met. It is quite unbelievable how it came together. It's still so amazing and seems like life was waiting for us to meet and when we did, life said "LET'S DO THIS!"

Breaking negative thinking is tough, but the best advice I can give is to start small. Don't know where to start? Here are some ideas . . .

1. Start small with your thinking. Try to turn one negative into a positive each day. If you tend to wake up in the morning and dread your day, try and change that thought to, today is going to be a great day and I'm going to treat myself to a Boston cream donut this morning (or whatever makes your inner child smile). From there, try to increase the positive thinking and take notice of what makes you unhappy. If there are things that make you unhappy, think about what you can do to eliminate them. Do you dread phone calls from someone? Maybe they shouldn't be in your life. Do you hate your job? Maybe it's time to look for a job you love. Start paying attention to what is creating these negative thoughts and assess the why. Start small so that you don't get overwhelmed and work your way up.

2. Write a list of your dream life and read it every night. This will help you define clear goals and dreams. When we were kids, we would wish for so many things and nothing limited us from dreaming. What happened to us as adults that we either became too scared to dream or felt like we weren't deserving? We all deserve love and happiness and if our crappy childhoods have taught us anything, is that life can be short. Make it the best you can!

3. Don't be afraid of disappointments. Having fear of disappointments is what limits us from dreaming and starting off the positive thought process. We are our own biggest roadblocks in life! Instead see that there is little risk to dreaming. What is the worst that can happen? They don't come true? Who said there was a timeline? If it doesn't happen today, maybe it will in a few weeks, months, years.

I hope this chapter gives you the courage to dream and wish for more in life! I'm sure not everyone will agree with my ideas on the power of thought, but really, what do you have to lose in trying? There is no risk, it's just your thoughts! I hope that you will start wanting good things for yourself and take the risk in believing you are worth a better life. I felt worthless growing up and taught myself to be small. I didn't think that I would be in a place where I could have more and didn't open myself to the possibilities of dreaming. I hope that you too will start believing you deserve more and wish for the life you want to have. As soon as I started thinking and wishing for a better life, my life changed. Your life can change too! Start dreaming and dream BIG!

Chapter 6

Who Are You In Relationships?

I had my first relationship when I was sixteen and it lasted until I was twenty-one. Peter was my first real boyfriend and one of the longest relationships I had as a teenager mostly because my Mom never scared him off. Peter was funny, sarcastic, attractive and a bit insecure which he covered up with humor. He had a big personality and a really good heart. He had dark hair and eyes, a built body and was obsessed with working out, always wearing tank tops to show off his biceps, wearing his baseball cap backwards. While we were young, I pictured him as being the father to my children and knew he would be a good Dad. I wasn't used to someone sticking around so long and not leaving. I will always have a soft spot for Peter for so many reasons. He was my first love and he taught me a lot. We had so many ups and downs, a few break-ups, and many arguments during the chaotic and confusing years of being a teenager. But we were growing up together. If I had to describe the relationship in one word, it would be passion (good and bad). We loved to fight, loved the chase, loved the drama but at the end of the day, we did truly love each other. In a way I was in awe of him as he had a bit of arrogance about him. He was unapologetically himself. Talk about the opposite of me. I was still working to be small and fading into the background and could be molded into any personality.

We met while working at my very first job. While some people would have been embarrassed to be working in fast food, I loved this job. It would take two hours to walk there or I had to take three buses (if I had money), but I didn't care. This job was freedom and a new start. I was in Grade 11, so I was fully recovered from my thyroid, although I was still known as bug eyes at school, unfortunately a name that stuck until the day I graduated. It was a fresh start away from my family and school. Most people my age hated working, I loved it! This job was a second chance with kids my age and I wanted to learn anything and everything.

I thought this was a great start for my exit plan away from my home life.

This was the job that helped me develop confidence. It was the first time I felt valued. My Mom didn't know anyone I worked with so, she couldn't tarnish any of my friendships. I met Peter after my first few shifts. He immediately started making fun of me, taking jabs at me! He told me to speed it up, to get out of the way. But it was in a fun way, where I would push back. The banter continued for a few months until he asked me out. Secretly, I would check the schedule to see when he was working and was excited when we had a shift together.

Not surprisingly, my Mom hated him, called him every name in the book and constantly tried to get me to break up with him. She used different tactics, such as guilt, criticism, and told me I was stupid and looked stupid for being with him. She didn't like his family and felt they were influencing my thoughts. I think her biggest hang up was she couldn't control the relationship and couldn't influence Peter's feelings for me. Peter avoided my Mom at all costs and did not like her at all. I used to joke that he was afraid of her (which he admitted!). She rarely saw him, so she was not able to influence him. He was the first person in my life to notice that something could be wrong with her and our family dynamic. He was the first person that I allowed to truly and honestly get close to me.

Peter always had my best interests at heart and taught me a few life lessons. What it felt like to be loved and wanted, that people could love me. To get out of my bubble and see the world. What a loving family looks like and that education is important. Peter was the longest relationship I had (friendly or romantic), so for the first time in my life I realized that I can have long lasting relationships and more importantly, that people can care about me and he would not leave me so easily. Maybe, I could be loved! By my teenage years, I was really convinced that there was something wrong with me and that nobody would ever love me after years of hearing mean things from my Mom. Peter and I didn't go to the same school, so outside of school we spent all our time together and couldn't get enough of each other. I always had a fear that he would leave me or worse, one day see that was I a bad person, just like my Mom had been saying. In fights, even if I knew he was wrong, I would ultimately forgive because I didn't want to lose him. We would fight a lot. We were intense and our relationship was addictive, and at the age of sixteen, I knew I wanted to marry him.

He knew most of what I went through with my family and after a few run-ins with my Mom, he stopped ringing the doorbell to pick me up and just honked the car horn. He, nor his family, could understand my family dynamic. I remember there was one day when he came into our house and noticed locks on our kitchen pantry and was horrified! I had to explain to him that my parents would lock up food because they felt like my brother and I ate too much. I was used to these locks. They had been on doors for as long as I could remember so I actually forgot that they were there! Instances like this, plus my Mom's treatment, pushed him to get me out of that house as much as possible.

Peter constantly challenged me and tried to get me out of my bubble. Travel and school were big priorities to him and his family. I had never set foot on a plane, much less anywhere outside of Ontario so it was intimidating. The first time I traveled was on a plane to Trinidad and Tobago where his extended family lived, and it was incredible! (Start small and local, right? Not me). It wasn't a resort or a "touristy" place. We were staying at Peter's uncle's house and really experiencing the city in Trinidad. What a big life lesson, to see the world and get out of your bubble. I once read a quote that reminds me of this trip;

"If you're not uncomfortable, you're not growing!" This trip was completely out of my comfort zone. It was so amazing to realize there are worlds out there completely different to your own.

The last life lesson from Peter was seeing what family should be. His family was very close and always encouraged Peter to be better. I practically lived at that house. We got along, although sometimes they questioned our relationship as they felt we were too serious, too young. They hated my family, and sometimes they wondered if I would be a bad influence on Peter. Can't say that I blame them as they were only looking out for their son. Peter was honest with his family and would sometimes share things about my Mom. There were times where my parents would lock me out of the house, and I would stay at Peter's overnight in a separate room. His parents were horrified and couldn't understand how my Mom could lock out a high school girl and not worry. I would often compare our families as polished vs shaggy! We came from two very different worlds, and at times I would feel like a homeless, unpolished girl! I do know his parents did care about me and wanted the best for me. Their concern was, how would I turn out given my unstable home life and how would it impact their son, which is completely fair as there was a lot of my family drama over the years.

I eventually ended the relationship with him when I was twenty-one. I felt like we were growing apart and going in different directions. I would always be thankful for those five years as the only consistent relationship I had in my youth and it taught me so much. Peter is now happily married with two kids and I couldn't be happier for him. I don't think he realizes the impact that he had on me but, having him in my life in the early years were my first few steps in getting my life together. Even though I didn't realize it then, he taught me some important life lessons. He taught me that people who do care about you, will do everything they can to stick around and fight for you. And they will not leave. While love can be complicated, it boils down to the simple things. If they love and want you, they will do everything possible to be in your life. For the most part, people will show you what they are feeling. You need to be open to read the signs. He taught me there are people who care about me, and there are real families out there that do care. He showed me the importance of travel, education and bettering yourself. I'm so appreciative for having him in my life for those years!

One thing I never admitted to myself or anyone else is deep down there was another reason
for ending things with Peter. He wasn't going to
save me anytime soon. I didn't see myself moving
out of my parents' house if I stayed with him. I
didn't see us living together in the near future. For
many years, he was a positive influence in so many
ways, but he too was on a path of finding himself
and the pressures I was going through were a lot
for any young guy to handle. I needed an older or
established guy to save me and get me out of the
crazy house living with my Mom (not something I
was proud of, but it was reality). While Peter was
on a proper path of what any twenty-one-year-
old should be living in a normal life, I was in cri-
sis mode and needed an escape. Peter's plan and
influence would have kept me at my Mom's for
many more years and I didn't think I was strong
enough to last that long. He was focused on school
and finding himself, as what was right. I was in
survival mode with the only goal of getting out of
my parents' house. I ended my relationship to find
a home. I felt I needed one asap.

My life after Peter got a bit chaotic. I wanted to
leave home, however I was not mature enough to
know what I wanted or needed in a relationship.
My next relationship helped me reach my goal

of moving out, but not much else. I got together with a chef with whom I worked at the restaurant and was eight years older than me. This chef was irresponsible with no real goals in life. Perfect (sarcasm)! We moved in together rather quickly. It was not a healthy relationship at all and slowed me down in terms of getting my life together. Unfortunately, two weeks after living with him, I called my Mom sobbing that I had made a mistake and asked if I could come back home. She said no. Imagine how low things must have been to actually want to move back home and then be denied. The day I moved out she was so happy. She cleaned my room around me as I was packing, working furiously to remove any trace of me living there. She couldn't wait to get rid of me. That phone conversation put me into a further downward spiral.

These were the years when I discovered weed, alcohol and numbed myself at any opportunity. I dropped out of college. I would go to work at the bar, come home with the chef and smoke up until I was an unfeeling blob of a person. We didn't last very long but after him, I had a series of relationships with men with deep seeded issues who needed fixing, or men that weren't interested in me, but I would keep chasing. It's like I was trying to punish myself and doing all I could to avoid working on myself. This was totally a distraction tactic. It's easier to worry and try to fix my boyfriend versus myself. A lot of partying and craziness happened during these years. Luckily, I met Michelle, who like Peter showed me I could be more. She was the only person that kept me going and refocused me on what my priorities should be, career and education.

Michelle exuded confidence and always took charge. She was a gorgeous blonde, sometimes crazy but in a good way. We partied a lot together, would rack up $600 phone bills from talking to each other all day every day. When we weren't talking on the phone, we were together smoking cigarettes, confiding in each other and dreaming of a better life. She had the drive and was a good influence in pushing me to get out of the bar industry and get a career. She tried to steer me away from the type of guys I kept dating. It's because of her I saw the light and got the strength to kick out the chef, which turned ugly. He stalked me for weeks after. He would leave pictures of me with a knife through my face for me to come home to. She supported and cared for me and would give me honest advice. We would pull all-nighters sending out resumes with the determination of getting a new job that could kickstart a career. I stayed in the bar industry for a few more years, landing my first office job at the age of twenty-six.

After Peter, I went on the self-destructive path again until someone intervened. Michelle helped me rebound from those years and get back on track. It's strange, the impact of abuse. It's harder and more work to want better for yourself than it is to concede to the notion of you are no better than what your Mom, the abuser, said. During my years of self-destruction, my Mom was ok with my life. I would hear a series of "I told you so's" about Peter and school. I realized the way that I grew up, made it hard work to be happy and so easy to believe I was the person my Mom said I was. I never once thought about not having a relationship with my Mom (because she was my Mom). I also still didn't really know who I was and was molding myself into whoever I was with. I didn't want to get to know who I was as a person. I was too scared of trying. That I would realize that I was a terrible person. My Mom's words "They are only friends with Jennie because they don't know the real Jennie" was the base of my fear. If I got to know the "real" Jennie, then I would want to end my life as she must be horrible. It was easier being a shadow and going through the motions. Burying myself in partying to numb my emotions and doing all I could to not be the freak I thought I was!

As morbid as this all sounds, want to know the biggest thing to take from these stories? I had someone rooting for me and pushing me to do better (first Peter, then Michelle, then my Gavin and our kids!). Somehow in the chaos there was always something good and positive. It was so hard for me to see past the darkness and appreciate the positive. I find this is usual practice for most people! I was so focused on my Mom but really there's a whole world out there and while she was the most important person in my life, she's only one person in this huge world. It's easier to complain than admit you're happy. It's easier to focus on loss than to dream. Why is that? When did life make us scared to dream and be happy? How do we allow ourselves to want more in life without fear of disappointment?

Developing relationships can be difficult when you don't know who you are as a person and don't have healthy relationships as examples. People can be oblivious to their dating patterns or even in denial. I know I was. But we all have some sort of pattern. Taking an honest look at yourself is a powerful tool to self-improvement and can be a challenge, especially if you are used to covering your imperfections. The interesting fact is that most people don't know who they truly are for they are too busy trying to look perfect. Or trying to cover up insecurities or bad behaviors by making excuses. Social media has amplified this even further. Only perfect poses or events are posted. It's not realistic and sets up false perceptions on what is a perfect life. For people who don't have a perfect life, it makes them feel inferior and like they aren't successful. Social media has intensified the competition in life when in reality, each of us are in different chapters, in different books, in different libraries of our journey and that's ok as we all need to go on our own pace! Learning who you are is the key to meeting the person with whom you are meant to be. If you don't know who you are or are pretending to be someone else, then how do you know what type of partner you need?

If you are starting to realize who you are, the next step is looking at your patterns in a relationship. Most people are not aware they have patterns, which is why it is so important to check-in on yourself to make sure that you are treating your heart in a healthy and honest way. Being real when it comes to how you interact and who you attract. A good way to check-in is to pretend your situation is that of a friend. How would you give your friend advice? Would you feel like your friend is being treated as deserved? We are all great at giving advice, however not good at taking our own. This is a great time to stop blaming your partner for relationship failures and start looking at yourself and taking ownership. Who do you attract? What are you looking for? Who compliments you? Do not be fearful to admit who you are looking for. Stop limiting yourself and stop settling for less. Try to know yourself as best you can and know who you are in relationships. And if you don't know who you are in relationships, this chapter will help you.

What is a relationship pattern? It's who we pick, how we interact with our significant other and how we allow ourselves to be treated. Some patterns start by looking at your parents or other family relationships. Some patterns can be created through attraction or even insecurities. Self-awareness will help you find who you are meant to be with.

Most people fit into one of the relationship patterns highlighted below. My hope is that you identify with one of these types and it gives you some clarity in discovering who you are. See if you fit into one of these types.

1. The Fixer-upper. If you tend to look for people who need help or are troubled so you can help them, you could be a Fixer. Are you attracted to the "bad boy" or to guys that are hard to get and show you indifference. These relationships tend to be unbalanced as the fixer is usually the responsible one and essentially looks after their significant other. How did you get this way? Many things could contribute to this. Did your parents have an unbalanced relationship? Was your Mom a Fixer? Or maybe there is some deep-rooted issue that you have from your childhood that makes you instinctively want to fix people? Maybe it is as simple as being the older sibling and you are used to taking care of things. This role can be exhausting as it is a constant job of trying to make the other person fixed. If you identify with this description, please try to remember, only you can fix yourself. Try to figure out why or how you got into this role.

2. The Alpha. You need to be in charge and look for people who are a follower or take a submissive role in the relationship. You hate being challenged in decisions you have made and like making all the plans. You like

the feeling of being in control. This pattern is more common than you think as sometimes the male simply wants to be taken care of (Mama's boy, anyone?). As this relationship progresses, you may find your significant other starts liking your interests and can lose their own personality, which may become boring to you. The challenge with this relationship pattern is that it can result in either the submissive person in the relationship snapping one day and looking for new found freedom, or eventually the alpha loses interest.

3. The Parent. (Most common if you are the oldest sibling in your family.) It is similar to the fixer, but with a few tweaks. This role has a mix of positive and negative traits, of being nurturing and overbearing. This relationship dynamic tends to put the couple in a role of parent/child unintentionally. It can lack in romance after time and make the person who is in the "parent" role feel resentful. The parent tends to treat their significant other as a child, constantly reminding them of their to-do list, and talking down to their partner. Have you ever heard of the term "whipped?" It can be a result of this dynamic.

4. The Codependent, giving up your individuality. Think of two people becoming one unit. You can become completely reliant on your significant other and lose who you are. There are some cases where people in this pattern start looking like their significant other as their style morphs together. You inherit your significant others interests and friends. This can be challenging because the changes can be very subtle over time and unless you are checking in on yourself, you may not realize that this is even happening. Are you the type of person that follows or leads? Are you too easy going? Easy going doesn't necessarily mean that you are codependent, just make sure you are happy being easy going and not giving away pieces of yourself to be with your significant other.

5. The Push/Pull. This relationship isn't balanced and very rarely on the same wavelength however, it can be exciting as there is an element of the chase. You might want to settle down and your boyfriend isn't ready. You thrive on the chase and excitement. This pattern has many peaks and valleys with lots of passion. However, with a lot of passion, it could result in lots of disagree-

ments and sometimes unhealthy traits (i.e., jealousy, resentment).

6. Balanced. This is the goal but requires steps to work on to get here. For you to achieve a happy, healthy relationship you need to know who you are first. Sounds easy, right? It's not. Knowing yourself means accepting the good, the bad and the ugly and taking a hard and honest look at yourself. Too many times we morph into people we think our significant other wants in a partner and lose ourselves. A healthy relationship means that you know who you are and that your partner loves you for your authentic self. Of course, there will be compromises needed along the way. But learn the differences between compromising and losing yourself. Compromising means both partners are making concessions to make each other happy. It does not mean changing who you are. True love means finding someone who loves your true self and vice versa.

Look for signs and don't make up signs. If someone doesn't call you back or doesn't want to spend time with you, look at it realistically and do not make excuses. People's actions are how to read what they are feeling. Stop feeling pressured to be in a relationship or that you need to get married by a certain age. Learn who you are first and the rest will fall into place.

These are the top relationship types. Don't feel you need to fit exactly into one of these boxes. You might be a mix of relationship types or as we are ever evolving, you might identify with different ones as you grow. Hopefully you might see a few traits that are familiar. The more aware you are, the easier it will be to find what makes you happy in a relationship. Learning who you are will help find what you are looking for in a significant other and what compliments your personality. Ensure you are dialed into who you are, or you might find you lose yourself in a relationship and not even realize.

To reiterate my advice on getting out of your relationship funk, fully investigate who you are. It's funny how little time we spend on self-awareness. We are more worried about what people think of us, creating an altered version of yourself. Who you are, is not your career, the number one answer people give. It's a description of yourself without limits. Grab a pen and paper and write who you are using descriptive words honestly. Now write a second list, who do you want to be? And write a third list by asking your closest friend to describe you and notice the differences. I would bet money that the list you wrote about yourself wasn't as complimenting as the list your friend wrote.

We are always our toughest critics and limit ourselves from our full potential. If you are feeling brave, write one more list. What is your dream life? It took me so long to figure this out. Again, we tend to limit ourselves and are scared to dream in fear of being let down. It's a way of not getting our hopes up. If you can't dream, and can't be fully aware of what you want in life, how can you strive to want more? When I started to learn about who I was and started wishing for a better life, that is when my life started taking off in relationships, romance and even my career. It's amazing when you discover who you are and the confidence that comes with it. You can get to where you want to be and then get the life of your dreams.

Here is an example of how to make your lists.
• Who am I?
• Who do I want to be?
• Friends description of me.
• Who do I dream to be?

To summarize this chapter, please remember these things.

1. Find out who you are as a person. This will help you build your life and find your partner. Write your lists.

2. Don't compare your journey to others. Everyone operates at a different pace. I was only ready to settle down at thirty-three, while being constantly reminded of my "clock." Nothing in life should be a comparison or a race.

3. Everything happens for a reason and trust the journey. If you want something hard enough and are ready, it will come but there is no time limit. Look at my story, had my first baby at thirty-four and got married at thirty-six. If I didn't go through everything I did, then I wouldn't have been ready for Gavin or my family. I am so appreciative of all I have been through, and I hope that this book helps you get there as well.

Chapter 7

Listen to Your Whispers! You Could Be Missing the Clues . . .

In my late twenties I was working at Pepsi as a sales representative and covering a route in a neighborhood that wasn't the safest. My job at the time was going to convenience stores and gas stations to sell Pepsi and take orders. While walking to my next store, a man stopped me on the street and asked me if I would be interested in being in an infomercial. I guess I looked skeptical as he gave me his card and told me to look him up and see that he is legit. If I was interested, give him a call. I looked him up, he seemed legit, so I met up with him. Because why not? It's not every day you are asked to be on TV! I met him at a restaurant (with friends secretly at the table next to us, you can never be too safe), to talk about this infomercial opportunity.

I rarely talk about my life story. At this age, I didn't talk about my life story as I was embarrassed about my family and ashamed that my Mom didn't like who I was. I was still playing the role of being "normal" and happy. This encounter was so odd. With this gentleman I found myself telling him things that I normally don't share . . . ever! He just had such a trusting, open vibe about him. After sharing some of my experiences with him, he mentioned another venture he was working on, a book by the name of *Making It In High Heels*. The book was a collection of inspiring stories from various women from all walks of life who had overcome challenges. It's purpose was to help young women going through troubled times and show them if you don't give up, you can turn your life around.

I guess it looked like I had my life together (I put on a good show), so he offered me the opportunity to write a chapter in the book. I wrote the chapter and it went into the editing phase, but unfortunately it never got published. You see, at the time I was trying to work on my relationship with my Mom which was constantly strained and when I mentioned this venture to her, she took it as an attack on her character. While my Mom was one reason for backing out of the project, to be fully honest I wasn't totally ready to share all my stories. I didn't think I was in any place to give advice as my "show" was all fake and on the inside, I was very depressed. I wasn't in the place I am today. I ended up pulling out of the book, which was released and became so successful that three more followed in the series. I didn't speak to that gentleman again . . . until recently, over a decade later.

Everyone has a purpose in life and even though most of us don't know what our purpose is, life has a way of hinting and pointing you in the right direction. If you are not ready to find your purpose, then you will probably miss the signs and they might be quieter than a whisper. Depending on where you are in life or how ready you are to hear them, they can be quiet and go unnoticed. Or if you are ready, they can be loud and obviously in your face. I have always had the thought that I was meant to help people, but being so insecure, I was never confident enough to try. It also seemed overwhelming as I didn't even know where to start! This year, I kept thinking about my journey, started listening to podcasts and audio books about people who made big changes in their life or had their life turn upside down. Listening to podcasts and self-help books was new for me. I never had any interest in the past. When I would resort to books or research, it was more scientific as I was looking for a quick diagnosis. I find self-help books contain a bit of magic and I didn't realize how much I would enjoy them and get inspired! One of the audiobooks, even mentioned the "whispers" and it really got me thinking, am I truly "listening"? I love my life, my family, my job. But was I meant to do more? Was I listening to the whispers? And it got me thinking about that book that I bailed on, years ago.

Literally the next day, LinkedIn reminds me of a birthday of a man. It happened to be the man that offered me a chapter in *Making It In High Heels* almost ten years ago. The timing was uncanny, and I couldn't believe it! I simply wished him a happy birthday and from there we started talking. That person was Sanjay Burman, CEO of BurmanBooks Media Group. I asked for a meeting, thinking maybe there's a project that I could work on to help people. Maybe he's working on another *Women In Heels* and this time I would not chicken out. He gave me a meeting which while I was thankful, I thought was a little odd as we hadn't talked in over a decade and I was the punk-kid who backed out of his book at last minute. Well here is the humbling and humorous part. He gave me a meeting because he had mistaken me for someone else. He had met someone a few months prior at an event and thought that I was that person. A fateful misunderstanding. Thank you to whoever that girl was! Without you, this book may not have happened. At the beginning of the meeting, I had to explain who I was and why I had asked to meet. I openly and honestly explained my thinking about whispers, how I was listening to podcasts and shared that I felt my purpose in life was to help people. We discussed ideas for a book and started talking about the possibility.

The point is that there was a series of events that perfectly lined up and got this book going or got me on this "path." The whispers being the podcasts, Sanjay's birthday plus the mistaken identity, leading me to writing this book. This happened within a few months, and a year later this idea of a book became a reality! The timing was perfect because I was more open and was re-assessing my life, asking how am I making an impact or helping people? What seemed like the impossible happened and this book is here! I've never written a book in my life. I don't feel like I'm any more special however, I was given this opportunity based on a series of chance events and because my thought process changed once again! It can't be coincidence. There is a reason I wrote this book, a reason you picked it up and are reading it. And I'm so grateful you did.

Everything happens for a reason and the reason for this book is the hope that it helps at least one person. This book was painful to write at times, almost broke me at others but the one thing that kept pushing me through was the hope that this could help someone. Are you "listening" for signs in your life? Have you ever had a feeling that you are meant to do something or felt like you were pushed in a certain direction? Now that you have hopefully begun to diagnose what you have been through, learned more about yourself, "scrubbed" your friends and family to remove the toxic ones, forgiven yourself and started treating yourself better. Start listening. See where life takes you!

Chapter 8

Letting Go

Mother's Day . . . this along with birthdays, were always a day of dread. It was the day of never doing enough, and no matter what we did, my brother and I were in trouble. I used to get anxiety over these days. This was a day when we literally prepared for battle. Starting when I was a kid, I would make cards for my Mom and no matter how much time spent or how many drawings it included, they were never good enough. She thought that there was never enough thought put into these gifts. One year I spent a month writing a poem for her (I think I was around eight), which I was so proud of and thought, ok this is it, this must have "enough thought." She read it silently, mocked it and ripped it up in front of me. When I was older and living on my own, living paycheck to paycheck, it meant taking her and my Step-Dad out to the Keg for a lunch, which usually cost over $300. The lunches were unsatisfactory because I didn't also buy a present. She had a long list of complaints and making her happy on these days was unachievable.

When I had kids, this didn't change. I didn't get a Mother's Day because I was so worried about her and trying to accommodate her demands. My husband's birthday falls about a week prior to Mother's Day. This was a problem. If there was anything else planned in the month, it usually created chaos. The year my little girl was born was no different. My daughter would have been approximately 6 weeks old when the dreaded day rolled around. My Mom decided she wanted to celebrate Mother's Day on Gavin's birthday and wouldn't budge. Gavin has a twin brother who lives out of town and they would always try to get together with his own family for this occasion. Plans were made for him to celebrate and I was not going to ask him to change that. So, I told her in the nicest way possible, trying to avoid a battle. Plus, I was so sleep deprived from having a newborn, I didn't have the energy for a fight. All I knew was that it wasn't fair for my husband to give up his birthday for no reason. I asked to keep Mother's Day on

Mother's Day and promised I would do whatever I could to make it special.

It didn't matter what I said, the fact that Gavin had plans was a problem and out of the blue she now mysteriously had plans on Mother's Day. That meant that we wouldn't see her at all if we couldn't accommodate her on Gavin's birthday. I said I was sorry to hear and to let me know if anything changed. Here's the thing about Gavin, he would do anything for anyone and never asks for anything. His birthday was not something I was going to give away for no reason, plus it just didn't make sense. It was her trying to cause conflict. At this time, she had only seen my daughter once, rarely asking about her grand-daughter (or grand-son for that matter). The last time she saw my daughter was in the hospital where she created so much drama over her birth.

My daughter was a scheduled C section so we knew that we would be in the hospital for two nights and had to find a sitter for my son. My Mom ended up trying to sabotage us getting a sitter by scaring people we asked to watch him, by using his food allergies against him. She never worried about me or my kids and this was no exception. Her only worry was her Mother's Day and her biggest point of contention was Gavin's birthday being a week prior to "her" day. She then messaged my brother to cover for her in case I spoke to him and asked about her plans. He was to tell me that my parents already had plans. She forgot one critical part, he was going to be in Singapore that day and my Step-Dad was supposed to drive him and his wife to the airport two weeks prior. Well, this caused another war which led my Step-Dad to not being allowed to drive them. Gavin ended up taking them to the airport and we didn't hear from my Mom at all on Mother's Day.

While I was worried about her, you know what I did? I slept and it was amazing! Gavin and my son made me a Mother's Day card, which was the best! I remember feeling sorry for my Mom as she created all of this drama and ended up sitting at home with my Step-Dad doing nothing and not seeing her kids. I could clearly picture how the day went, my Mom complaining how her kids didn't care about her and my Step-Dad sympathizing.

The last straw happened at a funeral a couple of weeks after the Mother's Day fiasco. My uncle passed away less than a year after my wedding. I mention my wedding, because he was so full of life on this day, always on the dance floor and the life of the party. His passing was a shock. He died from an aggressive form of cancer. We were all devastated, and my aunt (his wife, my Step-Dad's sister) was trying to be strong and hold it together on the day of his funeral. My aunt is a petite brunette with wire rim glasses. She is kind, selfless, hates drama and avoids it at all costs. (Sometimes I viewed this as a downfall, as there were times I just wished she would step in and help me). She has three kids who are adults now and have started their own families.

My Mom hated my aunt to the point of obsession, and this hatred included her three kids. Remember my baby shower, wedding etc? Anytime I wanted to invite my aunt to family get togethers, it was a battle. She didn't understand why my aunt had to be included since I knew how much my Mom didn't like her. To this day, I don't know where or why this hatred was there. My aunt always was a kind woman and to my knowledge never did anything against my Mom. My only thought is that it could have been jealousy. My aunt had friends, was content at her job of being a nurse and was overall just a nice person. I never listened to my Mom about excluding her, and instead fought the battle to include her in events. I had to re-assure my Mom that I would keep my aunt away from her. I have never heard one negative thing from my aunt. In fact, she may not even realize the extent of how bad this hatred was.

I was a little surprised when my Mom came to the funeral. She usually avoided events not about her. (Makes sense as NPD's hate occasions not about them). Seeing her there, I had a small pinprick of hope that maybe this was my Mom making an effort with the family. Forever the optimist, but I should not have been surprised when she tried to make it about her. My daughter was now about four weeks old and I was in my sleep deprived fog of a new mom. I did all I could to be there for my aunt and cousins, while avoiding my Mom. However, being so sleep deprived I'm not sure if I was any help. Even in my fog and being across the room, I started seeing the signs that one of my Mom's fits of rage was beginning to erupt. I noticed her glaring at family members and looking at my daughter longingly when my Step-Dad was looking. A storm was brewing. She started talking to Gavin together with my Step-Dad. Normally this would seem like an innocent interaction, however, seeing the signs leading up this, I knew something was about to go down. Normally I would have rescued Gavin, but I was with my aunt and cousins with whom I wanted to stay and support.

My husband filled me in on the conversation after we left. First, she complained about how much she missed her grand-daughter (no mention of my son) and wanted to know why I was keeping her from her grandparents. With the exception of Mother's Day (a.k.a. Gavin's birthday), she never asked to see her. Followed by complaining about how I never do anything for her on Mother's Day, this is after the fiasco we had just experienced. It may not seem big compared to some of the other things she's done to me, but it was my last straw. We were at my uncle's funeral where she should be worried about my aunt and focused on the family. She was the one who created the Mother's Day mess by trying to hijack Gavin's birthday. I was sleep deprived from having a baby and now she was trying to manipulate her lies to get my husband to feel sorry for her. Unbelievable!

In a strange way, I'm thankful for this occurrence. It got my husband to see her behavior firsthand. He had always believed me, but because some of the stories seemed a little crazy, I'm sure there was a part of him that worried I was interpreting things incorrectly. It was the last straw for me and my family. It was the day I finally said good-bye for good. I realized then and there, that no matter what I did I would never make her happy and she would never be there the way a Mom should be. If I wanted to have a happy life, be a good wife and parent, it was time to let her go. And I did. It wasn't easy, there have been a few times in my life where I missed having a Mom, especially raising two amazing little kids. But the key part was I don't think I had a genuine Mom who truly loved me and wanted me to be happy. Letting her and my Step-Dad go was freeing.

Freeing is a great word to define saying good-bye. When you have a toxic relationship with any person outside your family, you are encouraged to end it and are reassured that they are not worth your time or energy. When ending a toxic relationship with family, it's an experience that comes with some judgment attached.

The day I said good-bye I not only lost my Mom (who yes, was not a kind person but she's the only Mom I have), but I also lost some of my family as they were more worried about taking sides instead of worrying about my mental health, which was fragile. Losing my Mom was so difficult, and it felt like a death to me, which I still mourn to this day.

Saying good-bye for good was so final to me, so it was tough. No matter what she did to me, she was still my Mom and I knew I was going to miss her. I knew in my heart it was the only way I could be happy and protect my family, especially my kids, from her. When I did finally say goodbye, I didn't just cut things off. There will always be a small part in me that hopes she changes and a small part of me that misses the Mom on her good days, however few. I told her that I could no longer have her in my life unless she was open to go to family counseling with me because our relationship was not a healthy one. Deep down, I knew she would never go to counseling, because it would mean having to admit that something was wrong (which an NPD cannot do).

However, I thought if I put my relationship with her on the line, then maybe she wouldn't want to lose me and even give one session a chance. I was hoping that this news would shock her a little bit and make her realize how bad she has treated me and how much she hurt me. That maybe she would change to not risk losing me. Even before finding information on NPDs, I knew that she would view this as an attack, but I still had a small hope that maybe, that just maybe, she would try for me. This was the only way I could continue and while removing her from my life would be hard, I could no longer handle her verbal abuse, her gaslighting and her manipulation and I feared that it would start spilling onto my kids, especially my son. The day my daughter was born she made a comment that stuck with me. She was holding my daughter and said, "I'm so happy you had a girl. Boys are bad." It made me wonder if that's why she never bothered with her grandson over the years.

I wasn't surprised when she said no to counseling, viewed it as an attack and was followed by calling me every name in the book. Getting professional help was the only way I could continue having a relationship. Her response was full of narcissistic rage. She called me many names such as; princess, ugly (inside and out), spoiled, entitled, fat, gross, retarded, and wished that Gavin would see the real me and leave me. You name it, she said it. The name-calling shook me, and I said that this is a perfect example of why I can no longer have a relationship. If she ever changed her mind about going to family counseling, that I would go with her. This would be the last day that I would ever hear from her. Now, I knew that she would go on the attack because of the ultimatum, however I underestimated the fact that I would never hear from her again . . . ever.

I realize now that there was a small part of me that wished this conversation would have given her a bit of a shock and would have shown her that she needs to work on herself. I really wanted to work on things with a professional. No matter how bad she was to me, she's still my Mom. Also remember I just had a baby so my "Mom senses" were heightened. If my kids ever said they couldn't have a relationship with me, you better believe I would be camped on their doorstep and would do whatever it takes to keep them in my life. Hearing from relatives, she said she never tried reaching out to me because I changed my phone number. I've never changed my phone number . . . ever, same phone number for over fifteen years. This was my Mom's way of trying to get attention and of course, making it my fault. My Step-Dad is still a bit of a mystery as he would know that my phone number is still the same if he tried it, but he continues to ignore and enable her behavior.

Removing her from my life, I thought would mean a life with less drama and the journey of healing would finally start. This phase was supposed to be a fully positive one and a true awakening for me as I had cut out the person that made me feel small and worthless and encouraged me not to try because I wasn't good enough to succeed. I finally eliminated the toxic relationship that dragged me down my whole life. I could stop feeling guilty for never being good enough (or guilty for trying to be more) and start rebuilding.

This phase did change my life and it was freeing on so many levels however, I really underestimated two things. The mourning and guilt I felt, as I lost my Mom and the judgment that follows from others. Some people struggled to understand how I could have cut my Mom out of my life even after knowing a few stories. I thought that ending my relationship would be the hardest part but the questions and judgment that followed afterwards was just as hard. I found this surprising as it took me thirty-seven years to get to the point where I could no longer have this unhealthy relationship with her, and I didn't really cut her off! I wanted to go to family counseling to continue having a relationship. I found the judgment curious because my Mom had little to no relationships and always talked badly about everyone. I had spent years defending the family that now was too concerned about taking sides rather than being concerned for my wellbeing. I think my Mom needs professional help however as she is I suspect that she is an NPD, she will probably never accept the fact that something is wrong. If she had gone to counseling with me, it all could have been so different.

It took a while for me to find my footing with the judgment that I received, especially because I was still mourning the loss of my Mom and healing myself. I think people can't understand how hard this decision was, as I was the one that lost my Mom. And not by accident but by my choice. Sometimes when hard decisions are in your control, it's more difficult because it was your choice. While people will encourage you to stop talking to people who are mean to you and toxic, they will not encourage you if it's a family member, no matter how hard it gets. I was still hurting and healing, and honestly in need of support. Looking back, I realize that it's not up to anyone else to give support and make me feel better about my decisions. This was my decision and it's up to me to stay strong. The only thing that I found helped is simply telling the truth, which was also freeing as I was used to protecting her by hiding the treatment I was getting. For a while I still felt the need to protect her, but as time went on, I realized that it's no longer my job to protect her. It was time to protect myself and open up about my experiences. Most of all, to start healing and try to fully love myself. A lot of damage had been done.

Here is how I explained my decision.

1. I summarized why. I spoke honestly and told people that I suspected that my mom has a narcissistic personality disorder which

makes her mistreat me and verbally abuse me. This disorder makes her incapable of love and recognizing her behavior, which means she can't change as she doesn't see anything that she does is wrong. After going through my whole life being treated this way, I did the difficult thing of giving her an ultimatum, get family counseling with me or I need to say good-bye for good. She chose not to get the counseling. I realize people might not understand but, know this was one of the most difficult decisions of my life and I am hoping you can support me.

When you put it into terms like this, people may be a bit more receptive. For me, my biggest challenge was that I tried to hide her abuse for so long and always put on a happy face, so some people really didn't understand where it came from.

2. I asked people who knew my Mom, how did she describe me? As an example, most moms would brag about their daughter and their accomplishments. When I asked people this question, I would hear responses like, "Jennie only has friends because people don't know the real her." Or "You know

that Jennie can't hold a relationship, I'm not surprised" or "Yes Jennie did get that promotion at work, but I really hope that she doesn't mess this up like everything else she has, her boss doesn't know what he's in for," etc. This helped facilitate the conversation because when people would repeat how she would describe me, I would simply ask, is that normal for a Mom to say about her child? This is how I started getting some people to see that something was wrong and that I'm not being dramatic or lying.

It's been six years since I have spoken to my Mom and there are still some family members divided. I think I did the right thing and wouldn't change anything about my decisions. While I know it was the best for me and my family, it's still hard. I am working every day to remind myself that even if my Mom wasn't capable of loving me, that I am a good person and worth love.

I quickly touched on this earlier, however it looks like NPD runs in the family. My mother's sister has shown similar behaviors and has two daughters who also no longer speak to her for similar stories to mine. Daughters usually get the worst treatment from NPD Moms, but my brother stopped talking to my Mom partly due to how she was treating his wife. Given our family history and the fact that you now have four kids who have all stopped talking to their Moms for the way they were treated, you would think that people would be a little more understanding. This is partially the reason why I thought the decision would be easier. There is obviously something wrong with our family patterns.

I realized if people don't understand, it's ok as they may have had a proper upbringing and were raised in a healthy environment, that they couldn't even start to imagine a life otherwise. While it's ok if people don't understand, I still find it very interesting how we encourage people to get out of toxic relationships and fully support the separation needed, except when it comes to family. When a family is toxic, we're still encouraged to make it work and judged when we have to remove ourselves. What people don't realize is that we don't need the judgment, we are our own worst critics and the guilt is weighing. We need support and to be able to talk it out without feeling like we need to sell our choices. My whole life was built on trying to make my Mom love me and to make her happy. Transitioning to a life without her, meant that I needed to look at myself, something I avoided for so long and recognize that I am a survivor. Focusing on the judgment distracts me from focusing on what's important. My own mental health, healing, and FINDING HAPPINESS!

After letting my Mom go, the space widened with extended family as they were very concerned about picking sides. Maybe I didn't give this enough thought, but I never thought that this would be a problem. My Mom had alienated our extended family a long time ago. She rarely talked to them and insulted them a lot. In my twenties I reconnected with a lot of my cousins and would be the person to bring the family together, which she would ridicule constantly. This would be the same family that when I was younger my Mom would remind me that they aren't my real family (on my Step-Dad's side). I grew close to them though which was something that bugged my Mom to no end as she didn't like them and was very vocal about it to me.

I was the older cousin and the one the others would contact for help or if they needed anything and they weren't comfortable telling their parents. I loved that they would reach out as it made me feel like I was part of the family. In other words, when I said goodbye to my Mom, I thought that I would automatically get their support. This unfortunately didn't turn out to be the case. Instead I was accused of asking family members to take sides and every family get together was becoming too stressful. It's not that I asked family members to take sides, but I wished they were more thoughtful in the situation. If we were all invited to an event and my Mom was attending, to warn me ahead of time and if I choose not to go, don't get mad at me. I highlight these instances not to inflict blame, I understand it's hard for people to understand as she's my Mom. I want to show the aftermath and that part of my healing process is acceptance.

After I stopped talking to my Mom, she did start attending family get-togethers. Something she never did in the past. I would decline events and as a result, it got messy. The worst was a cousin's wedding where my parents came (the first wedding of any of my cousins that they actually attended). I did attend as it was a wedding and a once in a lifetime occasion. I wanted to go and show my support and celebrate the couple, however my Mom once again tried to divert attention to herself by crying in the bathroom and refusing to come out. She acted like the victim, cried to people about how I treated her. She wasn't there for the wedding, she was there to get sympathy and make it about her. That day made me real-

J. Patricia Gileno					171

ize that I needed to be open to the idea of family judging me for my decisions and no matter how much it hurt me or how betrayed I feel, I would need to be ok with the fact that they may never understand. The point of this though, is that my extended family are not bad people. In a way, I envy them for not understanding this situation as they never experienced anything like being raised by a narcissist. I worked hard to cover up my Mom's treatment of me, so a lot of them had no idea this abuse was taking place. In making the decision to remove a toxic person out of my life, I did it for me! Not for anyone else.

If you grew up raised by a narcissist, you may be used to this behavior and not even realize you may have others in your life that demonstrate narcissistic behavior. As I was insecure about losing people in my life, and then cutting my Mother off, it took me a while to really see which relationships were healthy and which were not. When I took a closer look, I found other unhealthy relationships where I was perhaps more forgiving for the fear of losing more people. I've since learned that it's all about quality not quantity. You may lose people, and face judgment however, this phase of rebuilding can be a positive one! Ensure your circle of friends are true friends and want the best for you. I gave examples earlier of my friend that would rather go clubbing than be there for me when I went through my break-up. Being raised by an NPD we are used to being treated poorly and accept it. Now it's time to realize that we are in control of our relationships and if people are not treating us in a positive and healthy way, it is ok to let them go.

It's time to look for all the good in life and stop accepting anything less.

When letting go, remember the following . . .

• Look for the good in your existing support system
• Realize that you have been covering the abuse for so long that some people will not understand and will judge.
• Everyone you meet knows a different version of you (There's a work you, a Mom you, a friend you etc.). Not everyone in your life can be treated the same but give some people a chance of knowing the real you and your real past.
• Sometimes people underestimate emotional or psychological abuse. If it's not physical, it may be harder to accept as you can't see the scars.
• Some people may never accept your choices.

- Take a good hard look at the people in your life. Do you see any more toxic people? It's ok to remove them as well, especially if you are like a magnet and attract them
- Remember that you are a survivor and there are more of us out there!
- It's ok to mourn the loss. No matter what, she was your Mom and this is tough!
- This is your life and you are in control. How do you want your life to look? Now is your chance!
- As hard as this is, it's time to stop wishing that your Mom was different and mourn the child who never had a Mom.
- Deep down you know what you're capable of, stop minimizing it! You are the only person stopping you!

Take a close look and identify people in your life that are doing more harm than good. Try to look and understand why they are the way they are (sometimes it's not about you) and determine if letting go is the healthiest option. While you can't control the behaviors of others, you can control your life and measure if what you feel is acceptable or unhealthy. For me, I honestly think I waited too long before saying good-bye to my Mom.

Chapter 9

Check-Ins

Took me a long time to realize, but I am discovering the amount of damage that has been done. I can be more sensitive than the average person and sometimes I tend to think worse-case scenario when it's not warranted. At times, it causes me stress and makes me feel overwhelmed and go "red" in emotion. I know what it is like to live life feeling the need to be invisible and not having any advocates and feeling alone. There are times when if I find out I haven't been invited to things, I take it personally (whether or not I even wanted to go!). I've also noticed that because I have worked so hard at being invisible the majority of my life, if I let someone in and they make me feel dismissed my emotional response may be stronger than warranted.

Writing this book as an example. This was a huge undertaking and because I never liked the spotlight, I felt like people would recognize how big of a deal this is as I'm actually opening up private stories and putting myself in the spotlight. Some responses to me writing the book in my eyes were dismissive or a lukewarm reaction. This Is the way I felt, something wrong with them? No! They probably have no idea how I'm feeling or how they reacted made me feel. On the flip side, I am also uncomfortable with being in the spotlight. Confusing right? Life has taught me that while it's tough to navigate through all of these feelings, the best thing I can do for myself is to be aware of how I'm feeling and "check-in."

One instance comes to mind was when I received a promotion at work. I told my brother about it and he was proud of me. We had company over, and he toasted my promotion to everyone. Seems innocent and "normal" right? Nope, not for me! A huge pit in my stomach formed because I was worried that people would think that "The world revolved around Jennie and that I had to make everything about me!"

My life has made me empathic to others and wanting to ensure I am inclusive. I am especially like this with my two kids. I try to be a part of their school, meeting their friends etc., as most parents do. But I can go overboard. I want to meet as many parents as possible so that I have their phone numbers. Seems great and that I'm a very supportive parent, right? I am, but it is based on the fear that if anything goes wrong at school, chances are I know the parents and can get involved. Most people don't think to the worst possible case, but I know how things can go wrong through my experiences. This means that I take everything to the next level, just to be safe. My son's birthday parties could reach almost one hundred people, as I would invite his whole grade. Yes, I know, crazy! I no longer do that, something for which my husband is very grateful!

Meeting all these families, I can see signs in some of the kids that are not receiving the attention they need at home and it's so sad to me. There are always signs, people just need to be more aware. And when I say people, I mean ALL people . . . families, schools, friends etc. While it's great how involved I try to be with the schools and the kids' social life, sometimes I tend to take on too much. Because I want my kids to have all that I didn't, and I want desperately for them to be happy and successful. I know I spoil them and working at a toy company does not help. Ultimately, I want them to feel like they are loved, supported and no matter what, they always have their family. Seems simple and it should be. I just need to support at a balanced level.

At work, we had an exercise to promote morale. With the greatest of intentions, for Valentine's Day the Mattel office put up paper hearts with each employee's name down a hallway. The ask was for employees to write compliments for that person on their heart. It's such a nice exercise and came from a positive place. However, the way my mind works, trying to forsee how things will make people feel, my immediate thought was about people who don't get anything written on their hearts. Flashback to my Grade 9 yearbook, when other kids would have full cover to cover signatures and wishes for a great summer, and mine was empty with a few half-hearted signatures plus a few "bug eye" comments. Embarrassing to admit, I signed my own yearbook a few times in different writing to prove to my Mom that I did have friends and that she was wrong in saying that people don't really like me. With visions of my high school yearbooks, I worried that there were going to be some empty hearts. So, I would stay at work late and fill up the hearts lacking in compliments in different handwritings to ensure that everyone felt the love. A person who had a stable upbringing probably always had full hearts and yearbooks and would not think about the possibility of empty hearts.

I can overthink scenarios and overanalyze how I acted in a social setting. I would analyze how others could perceive my words after a conversation and replay how I could have handled it better. I mentioned an example earlier of my boss once telling me that nobody is after me, everyone wants me to succeed and me being surprised. Those feelings of people wanting me to fail are not normal and are a result of my childhood. I know that now.

Noticing that my behaviors were not healthy and trying to be more self-aware, I created what I call check-ins. Every time I am feeling a strong reaction, I have trained myself to pause and assess. "Check-ins" are quick 5-minute internal connections to put myself in "check." Whenever I'm feeling mad, or invisible, or any strong type of feeling where I'm seeing red, I check-in on myself. I walk away from the situation (when I can) and ask, am I feeling ok? Am I being over-sensitive or over compassionate? Am I reacting according to the situation at a proportional level? Or am I reacting based on insecurities from my childhood? It may not seem like much, but I swear it works.

Just asking these few simple questions have helped ground me. I started doing this a few years ago and it helps me find balance. It is also a good way of being more self-aware and to see how you are interacting with others and ensuring that it is in a positive way. Most importantly, it is a way of checking in on my happiness and making sure this "super sensitivity" isn't too consuming and amplifying my emotions. (My sarcastic side also refers to these as the "Am I normal?" checks. Adding humor to things always helps no matter how bad the joke!). I find we are willing to go to doctors for health-related reasons, however we rarely check-in on our mental state. Try to check-in on yourself more often and take care of your well-being. Try to assess situations by looking at the full picture and not one dimensionally. Is the situation about you, or is there more going on?

I am now more self-aware, but it took me a long time to get to this place. I realize that I will always be a work in progress and for the first time in my life, I'm ok with that. I realize, that I think differently, and my thoughts can lead to negative ruminations more often than usual. I need communication and really worry if someone is too quiet and not telling me how they are feeling. I need to feel needed and am not comfortable in one-sided relationships so if someone is always about themselves and not interested in how I'm feeling or if someone doesn't let me talk, I see red. I have come to realize what these things have in common. I need to feel wanted. Being brought up in a house that was not full of love, it took me a long time to learn what is important to me and what are my triggers.

Try including check-ins into your day whenever you are experiencing strong emotions. It will help guide you and identify your triggers, strengthen your self-awareness and most of all, help. Don't over analyze, just check-in!

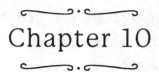

Chapter 10

Overview:
Where to Go from Here?

You've made it to the end! OR the new beginning! I hope this book has covered what you're looking for in your journey and the three steps are helpful to get you to your path to self-acceptance.

1. Recognizing when situations are not about you or in your control.
2. Identifying what happened to you.
3. Focusing on you and your self-improvement.

So now that you have come this far, what do you do? At this point, you should revisit what made you pick up this book and what were you hoping to gain from it. Find that piece of paper where you wrote and what you were hoping to gain from this book. Did you find the answers you were seeking? I bet you that through this self-discovery your goals have evolved and now you might be looking for something different. It's ok that it changed. We're constantly evolving and will continue to change and grow! What's your new goal and how are you going to conquer it? This chapter will provide a recap of everything that we've reviewed so that you have a cheat sheet to revisit as your goals change or evolve, you can quickly reference what we've learned.

I dealt with my complicated upbringing by avoidance, playing the role of being happy and "normal." Writing this book is the first time I have really thought about my life and the impact of my Mom's treatment has had on me. Let me tell you, there's no reason to stop being honest now, it almost broke me. Memories that I had suppressed and completely forgot about surfaced and emotions that I haven't felt in years came back. Now during this time, I was also experiencing a lot of stress from work adding to the stresses of writing this book, being a mom, and a wife. It was a lot to take on, especially for someone like me who wants everything to be perfect all the time. This year of writing was the exact opposite of perfect, but a crazy thing happened. I'm thankful for it. Once again, coming out of the chaos and stress something new happened. I learned more about myself and it helped me be stronger. It also helped me look at my life and once again "scrub."

Growing up my Mom always mocked people getting professional help and as you saw she chose not to get help with me when I asked her to. She felt seeing a therapist meant that you're weak and that it's an excuse to cry and be coddled. Well writing this book, I found I was crying almost every day and for the first time in my life I started seeing a psychologist. It was the best thing I could have ever done for myself. I didn't treat it as "an excuse to feel sorry for myself" as my Mom would say a lot to me growing up when I was sad (secretly I wonder if she didn't want me to seek therapy as it would expose a lot of her secrets). It was a way for someone to give meaning, definitions and tools for how I'm feeling. The psychologist explained that writing this book was a form of therapy called Narrative Therapy and it's a step to healing.

Narrative therapy is a form if psychotherapy that helps people find the skills and knowledge to help them conquer the problem they are trying to solve. While I found this book helped me deal with a lot, if I were to do it again, I would have started therapy at the beginning of this project. It didn't need to be as tough as it was. One way I managed a lot of my stress and feelings would be assigning a deadline. I love deadlines. It gives you an end date or a goal to chase after. This was a survival tactic I would use (i.e., I would tell myself; you have one day to be sad and then tomorrow you're going to pick yourself up and not allowed to be sad anymore). My first visit to the therapist I asked her how long this would take which surprised her. I explained my deadline theory and while there were positive attributes to it, she responded that healing mental health and maintenance is ongoing. There is no timeline to be sad or stressed. Life is a learning process. Your entire life.

This book started off by me giving advice and sharing personal stories so that the reader would trust that I know what I'm talking about because I've been there. This book is ending in a very different place. It's ending in a place that is embracing imperfections, being more self-aware, taking knowledge as power and using tools to navigate life because life is hard at times. This book is coming from an honest and true place and the realization that we will never be finished learning about ourselves, and that is a good thing to conclude.

Knowledge is power and if this book sparked similarities to things you have been through and provided some aha moments, take that as power. Now that you have an idea of what you experienced, maybe a few whys behind it, take this knowledge and do further research. Continue to educate yourself in your progress of healing and self-improvement. My one challenge to you is, try to be open about your struggles with your friends and family and be open to the possibility that you are a survivor and you can have a happy life. Try to stop being embarrassed or ashamed about your past and treat yourself for what you are . . . a survivor. If there are friends that are uncomfortable with how you're feeling and don't make you feel good about your discoveries . . . well, you know what to do!

This book was a big challenge for me as I've always been a private person, always playing the role of being "normal" and happy! I'm still terrified of publishing this book, but I'm trying to change my life and if that means in my journey I can help others change their life, then it's worth it.

Halfway through this book, I started getting cold feet, so I challenged myself. I posted something personal about myself on social media with the sole purpose of putting myself out there and sharing something that I'm insecure about. I have vitiligo on parts of my body, mostly my hands, knees and ankles. When I was younger, I was called "barf legs," as a teenager I would put pounds of make-up on my skin to cover and as an adult I would try to cover my white spots (i.e., hands always in my pockets). My vitiligo even affected me on my wedding day. I was relaxed about everything with the exception of my Mom and people taking pictures of my hands (you know the typical picture of the rings etc.). I told our photographer, if my hands were used in any photos, that they needed to be color corrected.

The reason I'm sharing this example is that this summer I posted a close-up of my hands, knees and ankles (no filter) on social media sharing my experience and sharing that I'm finally at a point in my life that I accept me for me! I have never put any sort of focus on my white spots and they just added to me wanting to fade into the background. I was so scared of the reaction, but I was trying to get comfortable about writing this book and sharing things about myself. With that social media post, an incredible thing happened! Comments of encouragement, compliments and an overpowering amount of love and support. I even had a few people that said thank you, that the post helped them with their own insecurities. If you have the right people in your life, they want you to be happy and want what's best for you! People who love you, want you to be happy and succeed (crazy, right?).

If my Mom had seen this post, it would have been mocked and followed by comments of, "it's always about Jennie. She always needs to be the center of attention." My whole life I was taught to hide and not be a nuisance no matter the circumstance and anytime I "shone" I was being selfish for one reason or another. Now I'm in a place of my life where I have surrounded myself with people who love me for me and want me to shine.

Now that you have your powerful knowledge, focus on the people who love you. If they really love you and want what's best for you, they too will want you to be happy and cheer you on as you embark on the journey of finding happiness and start accepting you for you. Take stock of your family and friendships and stop investing in people who don't want you to be a success or happy. Invest in people who love you for you, this is how normal friends and family operate. Seems so simple, however it took most of my life to realize. It is this simple and you do deserve love.

Everything in life is a choice. Now that you have identified that you are a survivor, stop acting like a victim and stop accepting bad treatment. When going through hard times, there are always choices which are in your control no matter what you have been through. You are in control of accepting that you'll be misunderstood, setting goals and striving for more, healing yourself, asking why things trigger you and continuously educating yourself.

You are not in control of everyone liking you, changing the past, changing other people (especially your Mom), some environments, however you can control how you react. Focus on what you can control, which is YOU! I hope that you take your new knowledge and use it to appreciate that you are a survivor and make the rest of your life amazing. It's your choice, as some people after abuse tend to fall into bad habits because they feel they are not worth anything more. This is your chance to start over and realize that every life (and I mean every life) has a purpose and that you are wanted. Now that you realize what you have been through, take that knowledge, acknowledge it, do your check-ins and wish for a better life. Wishing is the scariest thing you can do, but just try. You are worth more than you think. And you deserve an incredible life.

Now it's up to you! This book might be a lot to digest. I hope that it opened your eyes and gives you the courage to move on with your life. This book covered a lot . . .

- Removing the uncontrollable factors as you can't change them (i.e., childhood).
- Focusing on what is in your control
  - Relationships—What is your relationship pattern?
  - Trusting the journey
    - Everything happens for a reason
    - Power of thought
    - Listen to the whispers in your life
- Were you abused?
  - A look at bullying
  - What is Narcissistic Personality Disorder
  - Types of abuse and their impact
- Tools
  - Daily check-ins
  - Lists for reference
  - Relationship types
  - How to explain abuse
  - The power to dream

None of this is easy and you may be a work in progress for a while. The biggest thing I want you to get out of this book is the realization that you can have a good life and you deserve love. We all do, no matter where we come from! Start trying to find your happiness, your path to self-acceptance and kick ass in life!

CPSIA information can be obtained
at www.ICGtesting.com
Printed in the USA
LVHW021723230720
661378LV00017B/1602